DEFIANCE!

A Saga of David Crockett and the Alamo

James Charles Bouffard, Psy.D., Ph.D.

(Edited by: Lisa Diane Branscome)

Third Edition

Illustrated

Lynn Paulo Foundation
Pomona, California

ISBN 978-1-4357-5357-0

Printed in the United States of America

Other works by Dr. Bouffard:

Be A Private Investigator
The Magician's Fight!
A Quest For Absolute Power
The Entrepreneurial Ben Franklin

Dedicated to the Memory
Of
Lynn Vita Paulo

She defied a hardened world
— refusing to surrender —
until beaten into submission
by heart failure on
May 15, 1998
at the age of 65.

Rest in peace, Lynn!
You've earned it!

This work is also dedicated
to my sister
Mrs. Bill (Margaret) McManus
who found me
— she believes through Lynn's spirit —
after thirty years of looking.

I hope neither regrets it!

Acknowledgments

The author gratefully acknowledges Jefferson County Courthouse (Tennessee), Culver Pictures, Inc., Fort Mims Restoration Association, Crockett Cabin/Museum (Tennessee), the Center for American History, Facts on File, Inc., La Villita Historic Arts Village, the University of Texas at Austin, Texas State Library and Archives Commission, San Jacinto Museum of History, the Amon Carter Museum, the Daughters of the Republic of Texas (Alamo Library, San Antonio), the Center for Archaeological Research (San Antonio), San Antonio Light Collection and the Library of Congress for needed information and their kind permission to reproduce illustrations within this work.

To the staff of the Los Angeles Public Library, the library of UCLA and the smaller yet no less informative libraries of Claremont and Pomona, California for their amiable assistance and extreme patience, my gratitude is extended beyond mere appreciation.

Preface

In 1835, David Crockett's political career crumbled and he left Tennessee in search of a new homestead in Texas. But signs of war with Mexico brought him to San Antonio de Béxar, where he died in a defiant determination to live up to his legend. This singular gesture outstripped everything his bureaucratic promoters did to extend his reputation for fearlessness and integrity, leaving the final and most decisive act of legend entirely his own.

Historical documents, along with several edited versions of Crockett's biographies and autobiographies were scanned and re-scanned for accuracy, with cross-references deciding any discrepancies in facts.

While it is not my purpose to write a complete biography of David Crockett, I will make an attempt to clear up misconstructions surrounding his life — and of his death in a broken-down old mission known as the Alamo.

Such distortions undoubtedly emanated from Crockett's propagandized autobiographies, persisting through almanacs and "dime" novels of the day, and brought into the present century by a small school of wordsmiths disseminating erroneous information.

These works should not be read without some admonishment.

Especially is this true of ***Col. Crockett's Exploits and Adventures in Texas, by David Crockett***, which could hardly be accepted as genuine.

Exploits, added posthumously to Crockett's life story in 1836, was actually created by hack writer William Penn Smith for the publishing firm of Cary & Hart in Philadelphia.

As the tale goes: David's diary was found on the Alamo grounds following the massacre and sent to Alex J. Dumas from Charles T. Beale to arrange for publication.

Supposedly poring over the diary, Smith produced an entire manuscript for Cary & Hart — as tradition has it — overnight.

A spurious affair to say the least, historical inaccuracies glared from nearly every page of ***Exploits***, yet the duplicity went unquestioned for 120 years. Even one of David's descendants contended to the authenticity of his grandfather's diary, and to ***Exploits*** undeniable credibility. Likewise, Walt Disney Productions drew upon the book for its ***Davy Crockett at the Alamo*** installment of ***Davy Crockett, King***

of the Wild Frontier 1954-55 television series.

No evidence marking the existence of a "Crockett diary" has ever been substantiated. Moreover, the names of both Dumas and Beale have proved fictitious in this instance.

Therefore, let's stick to the facts as best we can by dismissing ***Col. Crockett's Exploits and Adventures in Texas*** as a reliable source pertaining to the Alamo siege; by padding softly through ***A Narrative of the Life of David Crockett of the State of Tennessee, Written by Himself***, ***An Account of Col. Crockett's Tour to the North and Down East***, and by gliding cautiously through various documented material found on David Crockett and the Alamo.

It is, of course, certainly an author's prerogative to use conjectures or theories when chronicling the past — as long as the theories advanced are within the realm of plausibility. Writers reporting historical happenings need to inspect all evidence critically before drawing their conclusions. And must, above all, remember that everything in print is not necessarily correct.

Ultimately, if this recounting directs even one future author to a reality that writing biography or history is more than benightedly following his or her predecessors, I shall be amply rewarded.

Dr. James Charles Bouffard
Pomona, California
March 17, 2008

“His favorite costume was a coonskin cap and buckskin jacket. It is assumed that he wore trousers of some sort, although they are never mentioned.”

Richard Armour on David Crockett

It All Started With Columbus

(1953)

Contents

Part Three
The Alamo, Death…and Victory

Miscellaneous

Illustrations List

Following page 210:

Illustrations List

Part One

Ancestral Past, Birth...and Adventures

Prologue

During the reign of King Louis XIV, Huguenots were banished from France.

Under Louis III, this Protestant sect flourished; their religion respected, their gentle manner often admired. But, in 1672, the papacy stepped in to reclaim France for Holy Rome.

"She is Catholic, and must always remain thus!" thundered Pope Clement X from his seat in Vatican City.

"If it please Your Majesty," addressed a tall, handsome, 29-year-old man to his king.

Louis sat on his thrown, his chin resting on whitened knuckles, his eyes heavily lidded. Although a pleasant member of his Court, Antoine Crocketagni's repeated haranguing grew tiresome. They were useless arguments at any rate. The decision to oust the Huguenots had already passed through parliament.

"To exile a poor religion to accommodate that of a wealthy one is oppression. My wife and I became Huguenots not just as a protest against a religion with gold-laden doctrines, but to help France see…"

"Blasphemy!"Bishop Tomas, sitting in attendance, vaulted to his feet. "Who is this man? How dare he criticize the one religion sanctioned by God Himself!"

The bishop sat down and straightened his miter. Louis startled awake.

"All holy religions are sanctioned by God, sir!" shouted Crocketagni, unable to control his anger. Here sat the man who sent his priests traveling the countryside selling prayers for gold coins. If a citizen, or even the poorest of peasants, refused to help replenish Church coffers for redemption, their soul would find itself condemned to a stay in purgatory. Or worse, to everlasting hell!

The bishop sputtered, his face red with fury.

Louis XIV raised a royal hand.

"Antoine," he spoke softly, as if to a brother, "we have always liked you. But, alas, the matter has already been settled. The ships are loading for England even as we speak. There is nothing we can do about it."

"But, Your Majesty…"

Raising his hand for silence, Louis continued in a sympathetic yet firm voice.

"The matter is closed, Antoine. If you and your wife will renounce your new, deceptive, religion and come back to the True Church, everything will be as before. The Court will be happy. We will be happy. But to resist our counsel would prompt…"

"Expulsion!" exclaimed Bishop Tomas; springing up with such excitement his miter fell to the floor, his baldpate exposed. Frantically grabbing for the rolling headgear, he replaced it and sheepishly resumed his seat.

"What do you say, Antoine?" Louis stifled a chuckle. "Will you stay with us? Or will you follow that insidious group to a forbidden country?"

"That insidious group as you call it, sire, is disposed to forsake all they know for their beliefs. Would that gentleman," Crocketagni wagged a contemptuous finger at the bishop, "be willing to do the same. Hence…"

"Blasphemer! Blasphemer!" the bishop fumed.

"Hence," Crocketagni went on, his eyes cast downward, "I will follow them. Sad though I am to leave my king. Perhaps someday all religions will come together as one. With no one religion subverting the other."

"Ah well, Antoine," Louis sighed, ignoring a smirking Bishop Tomas. "Perhaps someday, though not today. We will expect you and your family away from Court by nightfall."

So a defiant Antoine Desasure Perronette Crocketagni, with his wife Louise DeSaix and infant son Gabriel, left the luxurious Court of King Louis XIV for a little village in southern England.

From there they moved to Ireland.

Antoine changed his name to Anthony Crockett in order to relinquish his French connection and cast a family crest of a wild gray goose, entrusting it to following generations.

The wild gray goose!
Renowned for its strong flight against the wind…

"In all the disputes which have excited Christians against each other, Rome has invariably decided in favour of that opinion which tended most toward the suppression of the human intellect and the annihilation of the reasoning powers."

Voltaire
(Francois Marie Arouet)
French poet and writer
(1694–1778)

Chapter 1

On August 17, 1786, Rebecca Hawkins Crockett, gently caressing the newborn infant sleeping peacefully beside her, smiled up to her husband.

John Crockett returned the smile, but felt troubled. Eastern Tennessee, then encircled by conflicting Cherokee and Creek tribes, was in constant danger of Indian attacks. His own parents had been killed, with one brother wounded and another captured. Perhaps he should move his family to a less troublesome land.

Rebecca disagreed.

"John," she cuddled the baby closer. "You'll keep our family safe. I know it. And nothing will happen to little Davy here as long as I have breath."

So the matter was closed for the present.

John Wesley Crockett was born in 1754, migrating with his parents and brothers from Maryland to the farmlands of

Pennsylvania, later joining in the battle of Kings Mountain during the Revolutionary War. After the war he moved for a short time to Lincoln County, North Carolina, then followed his parents and brothers into eastern Tennessee.

Rebecca Hawkins was born and raised in the newly incorporated state of Maryland. She and John met, married, and started a family of three girls and six boys — of whom Davy was the fifth. Davy was born near Big Limestone Creek, which flows into the Nolichucky River in Greene County, Tennessee.

They lived a poor, miserable existence.

By 1793, John determined he and his family had had enough of starving and scraping.

Besides, Indian attacks were increasing. There neighbor, living a distance of only five miles, recently lost his wife and child, his cabin sacked and burned to the ground. The marauding was too close for comfort.

This time Rebecca agreed to the move.

So, packing their meager possessions and the children into a rickety old wagon, hitching Ol' Jenny to the front and their one milk cow to the back, off they went. Davy, aged 7, sat facing the rear of the wagon, watching with longing sadness the cabin of his birth fade into the distance.

Their new home was Cove Creek, Tennessee, where John went into partnership with a Thomas Galbraith to erect a water mill. Unfortunately, before completion of the mill, a freshet [1] swept away everything — including John's small investment — and nearly drowned the family.

Gathering what soaked belongings they could manage, they trekked out of Cove Creek to what is now Hamblin County, Tennessee.

There, resting on the Knoxville–Abingdon Road in the forested section of Morristown, John and Rebecca decided to erect a tavern on the spot.

They were poorer than they had ever been in their lives.

In 1798, an old Dutchman named Jacob Siler, driving a herd of cattle from Knox County to Rockridge, Virginia, stopped at John Crockett's Tavern. He was in need of help to continue his travel to Virginia. Could the tavern owner spare one of his sons? The pay would be handsome.

John Crockett, ever in need of money, called for 12-year-old Davy.

In agreement, John was to receive half-pay now, Davy to collect the remainder upon reaching their destination.

While Siler and John finalized the contract with a handshake and a drink, Davy reluctantly prepared to leave home for the first time.

The old Dutchman was a friendly sort. Throughout the four hundred mile journey, everything went well. But Davy — as is the want of a boy not yet in his teens — was home sick. He wished to see his family again. Including his father, who had raised a heavy hand to him on several occasions.

Siler beseeched the boy not to leave.

"I deplore such treatment by a father," he said. "You should never go back to that wretched family."

Fearing the old man for reasons he did not quite understand at the time, Davy accepted to stay but made plans for an escape.

Which wasn't easy.

Siler vigilantly watched the boy during the day, locking the door to his room at night. This, coupled with a yearning to see once more his mother and father, made nights sleepless. Days filled with anxiety.

One day, while enjoying the rare pleasure of frolicking with two neighboring boys, Davy spotted three wagons ambling up the road.

Recognizing the driver of the lead wagon as a frequent visitor to his father's tavern, he turned for any sign of old Siler. Not seeing him, he hailed the wagons and acquainted the three of his plight.

Dunn, listening to the boy with earnest, said he and his sons — who were driving the other two wagons — would be spending the night at a tavern seven miles down the road. If Davy could get to them before daybreak the next morning, they would take him home.

Three hours before daybreak, Davy left Siler's house into a heavy snowfall. Already the powder was eight inches deep, threatening to seep through his homemade boots.

Ignoring the growing numbness to his toes, he faced in the direction of what he hoped would be the road. Visibility remained a shadow in the snow-covered moonlight.

Davy wondered at his luck. His keeper had actually forgotten to lock him in on this, of all nights.

Pitching forward as the ever-thrusting snow attempted to force him back to the Dutchman's waiting abode, his young heart pumping with an eagerness for freedom, he pressed through to what appeared a road. Snow covered everything. The only indication there was even, or ever had been, a road was an opening in the trees large enough to allow for trafficking of wagons.

Stopping to catch his breath and bearings, he turned toward the course Mr. Dunn and his sons had taken the night before. Strangely, now that he was away from the house by a good half-mile, the falling snow slowed until there was no more than a periodic flake drifting to the ground. Moonlight brightened the countryside.

Young Davy Crockett was headed home.

"Out of the dreariness,
Into its Cheeriness,
Come we in weariness,
Home."
Stephen Chalmers
American poet and author
(1880–1935)

Chapter 2

"A 13-year-old boy ought to be in school!" stern-faced Benjamin Kitchen admonished John Crockett about six months after his son returned home.

In those days parents decided whether their child should attend school and John had decided long ago that Davy was "too quirky for schoolin'."

"He's a crack shot with a rifle. That's all th' learnin' he needs."

But the schoolmaster's reasoning won out, with the help of Rebecca.

"If Davy learns t' read an t' cipher," she gave her husband a sly grin, "he'll be of more worth t' th' tavern."

So Davy Crockett went to school — for 4 days.

"I went four days," Davy tells us comically in his own words, "and had just begun to learn my letters a little when I had an unfortunate falling out with one of the scholars[students] — a boy much larger and older than myself. I knew well enough that though the school-house might do for a still hunt, it wouldn't do for **a drive**, so I concluded to wait until I could get him out, and then I was determined to give him salt and vinegar.

"I waited till in the evening, and when the larger scholars were spelling, I slipped out, and going some distance along the road, I lay by the way-side in the bushes, waiting for him to come along. After awhile, he and his company came along sure enough, and I pitched out from the bushes and set on him like a wildcat.

"I scratched his face all to a fritter jig, and soon made him cry out for quarters in good earnest.

"The fight over, I went home, and the next morning was started out again for school; but do you think I went? No, indeed. I was very clear of it; for I expected the [school] master would lick me as bad as I had the boy. So, instead of going to the school-house, I laid out in the woods all day until the evening when the scholars were dismissed, and my brothers, who were also going to school, came along, returning home. I wanted to conceal this whole business from my father, and persuaded them not to tell on me, which they did.

"Things went on in this way for several days; I starting with them to school in the morning, and returning with them in the evening, but lying out in the woods all day. At last, however, the master wrote to my father, inquiring why I was not sent to school.

"When he read this note he called me up, and I knew very well that I was in a devil of a hobble, for my father had been taking a few **horns** [corn liquor], and was in good condition to make the fur fly. He called on me to know why I had not been to school. I told him I was afraid to go, and that the master would whip me, for I knew quite well if I was turned over to this old Kitchen, I should be cooked up to a cracklin' in little or no time. But I soon found that I was not to expect a much better fate at home; for my father told me, in a very angry manner, that he would whip me an eternal sight worse than the master if I didn't start immediately to school. I tried again to beg off, but nothing would do but to go to school.

"Finding me too slow about starting, he gathered about a two year old hickory, and broke after me. I put out with all my might, and soon we were both up to top speed. We had a tolerable tough race for about a mile; but mind me, not on the school-house road, for I was trying to get as far t'other way as possible. And I yet believe, if my father and the school-master could have both levied on me about that time, I should never have been called upon to sit on the councils of the nations, for I think they would have used me up. But fortunately for me, about this time I saw before me a hill, over which I made headway, like a young steamboat. As soon as I passed over it, I turned to one side, and hid myself in the bushes. Here waiting until the old gentleman passed by, puffing and blowing, as though the steam was as high enough to burst his boilers.

"I waited until he gave up the hunt, and passed me back again; I then cut out…"

Davy kept on going.

The year was 1799. The new country — that year — would reel with the loss of Father Washington.

Rebecca would cry for the loss of her child.

Brothers and sisters would mourn as if he were dead.

John Crockett stood by the door each night throughout that year, expectantly awaiting return of a wayward son.

Chapter 3

In 1802, a buckskin-clad youth cautiously entered John Crockett's Tavern.

Suspicious eyes followed the panther-like form easing to an empty corner of the room. The stranger sat down and placed his hunting knife on the table.

Rough men grumbled for fear of trouble until Betsy Crockett jumped from her seat, ran over, and hugged the new arrival so fiercely about the neck he nearly toppled from his chair.

"Here's my lost brother," she shouted.

In the more than two years he had been away Davy had changed so much — in height and width — no one, not even his mother and father, recognized him. But Betsy so loved her younger brother; his face remained a picture in her mind from the day he left.

"My feeling," he wrote, "at that time it would be vain and foolish to describe… The joy of my sisters, and my mother, and, indeed, of all the family, was such, that it humbled me, and made me sorry that I hadn't submitted to a hundred whippings, sooner than cause so much affliction as they had suffered on my account."

Within a week of Davy's return, John motioned his son aside and asked a favor. He was short of funds and in debt for $36 to a surly drinker and gambler named Abraham Wilson, who would just as happily cut a man's throat for the sum of two dollars.

Davy agreed to work for the man until the debt was paid off, and six months later handed his father a note discharging the obligation.

John Crockett was on a roll. He then pleaded to owing money to a Quaker farmer named John Kennedy, imploring his son to work off an amount of $40.

Davy shook his head in disbelief.

"You cin then go your own way," promised John.

Six months later the second liability was cleared, and Davy continued working for Kennedy as a hired hand.

Old Kennedy would soon introduce Davy to his niece, a vivacious young girl named Linda, with whom he found himself "head over heels" in love. Finally, following agonizing months of "acting the fool," he screwed up enough courage to ask for her hand in marriage.

Unfortunately for this love-stricken young man, she had previously given it to her uncle's son and he had just experienced his first disappointment.

Angered though he was, he would seize this opportunity to reconsider his life to this point.

Who could blame Linda her choice, he mused? What beautiful woman would want a man with "so li'l learnin' "? Even now, at seventeen, he could not read a book; nor "copy the first letter of the alphabet."

And so it was that Davy Crockett went back to school. Perhaps not long enough for consideration as a well educated gentleman of the day, yet sufficient to tumble innuendoes, whispered and spoken aloud during his lifetime and after, that he was nothing more than an illiterate.

Still, he yearned to be married.

In 1805, educated and well dressed, he courted Margaret Elder.

The wedding day was set for a Thursday, and young Crockett had been beside himself with joy for weeks.

However, five days prior to this happy event the girl's sister set him down and informed him in a somewhat gleeful key that his "future wife has changed her mind" and intended marrying another.

Without saying a word he slowly pulled the marriage license from his pocket, tore it in half, picked up his rifle, and shambled from the house. "I was only born for hardship, misery, and disappointment," he sadly reflected. "I now began to think that, in making me, it was entirely forgotten to make my mate; that I was born odd, and should always remain so, and that nobody would have me."

In this melancholy state, Davy entered a shooting contest

that afternoon.

Facing the target at some 200 yards, tears clouded his vision. Raising his rifle, he wiped his eyes with the forefinger of his left hand and aimed at the hazy mark. A visage of Margaret Elder appeared through an esoteric mist, the ball slamming blackness between its pretty orbs.

Davy had never been as angry in his life. He won the match hands down. Each shot a bull's-eye.

Mary "Polly" Finley, however, would mend his heart in the spring of 1806.

Meeting at a harvest dance, a whirlwind courtship soon followed. The pretty red-haired lass was as captivated with Davy, as he was with her. "No one," he wrote, "will take my Polly away from me."

Yet Polly's possessively Irish mother, having someone else in mind for her daughter, frowned. This Crockett character was a "typical Irish fighter," with a knack for getting into scrapes. She knew stories…

But Polly's father decided, then and there, that Davy and Polly were a match. No arguments. No questions. His consent had already formed into words.

In August of 1806, Davy and Polly were married, setting up housekeeping on a small rented farm not far from the Finley house.

In 1807, their first son, John Wesley, was born. In 1809, number two, William, arrived.

"We worked [the farm] for some years, renting ground and paying high rent, until I found it wasn't the thing it was crack'd up to be, and that I couldn't make a fortune at it just at all. So I concluded to quit it, and cut out for some new country. In this time we had two sons, and I found I was better at increasing my family than my fortune. It was, therefore, the more necessary that I should hunt some better place to get along; and as I know'd I would have to move sometime, I thought it was better to do it before my family got too large, that I might have less to carry."

In the latter part of 1809, Davy and his family — along with one old horse and two colts — made their way to the open Elk and Duck River country, over the Cumberland Mountains in southern Tennessee.

It was here that Davy began distinguishing himself as a hunter. Here, too, began ***the legend of Davy Crockett***: Stories still told today around campfires of Tennessee, Kentucky and the far-reaching Ozark Mountains.

And here — he was to make his first small fortune.

Wild turkey, possum, raccoons abounded the region, and anyone wily enough to outsmart these creatures found their pockets jingling with coins. Coonskins over a hunter's shoulder traded for sugar, flour, whiskey, and even a side of beef.

Though considering himself a bear fighter, Davy "set t' learnin' ev'thin' I could 'bout these li'l varmints."

It paid off.

Within months the countryside hummed: "Davy Crockett cin outsmart most any coon or possum."

"Why Davy cin grin a coon right out'n a tree, sure as yir

please," remarked his neighbors.

In 1811, having accumulated a sizable nest egg and tiring of "small game," Davy talked Polly into moving to the black bear country of southeastern Tennessee. He had plans for a new business venture. Selling bearskins for rugs.

In 1812, a daughter Margaret entered the world "as cute as a button and twice as round."

Holding the infant in his arms, he laughed, "Maggie, m' love, yir country bumpkin is gonna make us all rich."

Was he thinking of his one time love for Margaret Elder?

While Davy and Polly worked to increase their chances for an improved home life, trouble brewed below Tennessee's southern border.

Tecumseh, superior chief of the Shawnee Nation, urged tribes from the Great Lakes to the Gulf of Mexico to unite and drive "the white invaders back from whence they came, upon a trail of blood."

His plan combined bringing together a warlike confederation whose sole purpose would be the extermination of white settlers in the south, then join forces with the British for annihilation of the remaining northern whites.

England had pledged assistance in both the northern and

southern states and territories, and promised to hold the country for Indians alone after the war.

Tecumseh was killed in the Battle of Thames on October 5, 1813, while supporting the British.

Thirty-six days earlier a half-breed known as Chief Red Eagle (William Weatherford), leader of militant Creeks in the Mississippi Territory, formed a war party in support of Tecumseh.

On August 30, 1813 they attacked Fort Mims in southern Alabama, massacring nearly every white man, woman and child.

Of the 553 human beings occupying the fort, only thirty-six survived. Among these were several blacks spared to serve as Creek slaves, a half-breed woman and her children, and ten settlers — led by a Dr. Thomas Holms — who fought their way to safety.

General Andrew Jackson received orders to suppress the uprising.

The Creek War had begun as a spiraling agenda to the War of 1812.

Polly Crockett fearfully moaned.

Terrified of what would become of her and the children should anything happen to her adventuresome husband, she begged Davy not to join Jackson's army of volunteers.

"But what would happen t' us all," he wiped tears from her cheeks and kissed her gently on the forehead, "if we don't put a stop t' it? Th' Indians will be all about, scalpin' th' women an' children, until we are all kilt in our own cabins. Anyhow, I must go!"

Polly cried a little more. Then returned to her work. She knew there was no stopping her headstrong husband once he had made up his mind.

Davy kissed the children, gathered his rifle and gear, kissed his wife on top of the head — which she seemed to ignore — and strode out of the cabin to his waiting horse.

Both man and animal must have questioned their sanity as they rode off to war.

Chapter 4

Muster took place at Winchester, Tennessee, a small settlement ten miles from Davy's cabin. About ninety men were assembled when he arrived and dismounted. Like him, most of the men had ridden in on their own horses, carried their own rifles, wore coonskin or fox skin caps, hunting shirts, buckskin leggings, and moccasins.

Lawyer Francis Jones, later a congressman from Tennessee, addressed the excited assemblage.

"Do we all want to fight Indians?

"Yes!" howled a resounding, synchronous reply.

"Then sign up and get to it! The Red Sticks [1] will rue the day they started their bloody butchery!"

Surging forward, rifles punching air above their heads, Davy followed the exuberant 18-year-old son of Major William Russell.

By nightfall, a total of twelve hundred volunteers enlisted under the command of Colonel John Coffee.

General Jackson, not yet arrived from his headquarters in Nashville, would command the entire army.

Jackson had been personally delayed in making his way south, so Coffee and his men moved on their own toward the Creek Nation.

Riding into Alabama they crossed the Tennessee River and set up camp on an overlooking bluff, where Coffee called for scouts to survey Indian movements.

Accepting the assignment under the command of Major John Gibson, Davy, young George E. Russell and ten others cautiously moved out.

Re-crossing the Tennessee River to a place called Ditto's Landing, they furtively penetrated enemy country.

There, Major Gibson divided his small band into two sections. Davy and Russell would lead the one, while Gibson took the remaining five. They were to reconnoiter the area, then reassemble before dusk.

Although Davy and his men returned shortly after nightfall, Gibson's detachment had not yet arrived. So the seven anxiously followed the major's route along a thin path to an empty Cherokee village, then to the cabin of a man named Radcliff.

Radcliff denied knowledge of the men they were seeking, but warned of seeing ten Creek warriors not more than an hour before.

"Go back," he urged. "If you're caught here, we'll all be

killed!"

Five of the men, favoring Radcliff's entreaty, elected to forget about Gibson and return to the safety of Colonel Coffee's camp.

Angrily siding with Davy to move on, George Russell offered to shoot the first man attempting a retreat.

Reluctantly, the dissenters accompanied their leaders out of the woods to a camp of friendly Creeks.

The ten warriors mentioned by Radcliff were not seen.

In the Creek camp, Davy had hoped to learn the whereabouts of Major Gibson and his little group, along with any movements of a war party.

The Indians were silent to both questions, yet tendered a meal and lodging for the night.

As Davy and his men prepared to bed their horses, an Indian runner whooped in with news of a party of Creek warriors — numbering more than a thousand — gathering at Ten Islands to meet General Jackson's forces.

Thanking the Indians for their friendship and hospitality, the seven re-saddled and raced to cover sixty-five miles to the volunteers' encampment. This report must reach Colonel Coffee without delay.

Pounding into camp around 10 a.m. the next morning Davy pulled his mount to a halt, landing on the ground sooner than his horse's front legs; his men drawing up behind him. Waving Russell and the others on to breakfast, he excitedly plunged into the colonel's tent.

Coffee listened with little interest, suggesting the scout

get something to eat and a little rest.

Davy left the tent confused. He was sure his information was important, yet the colonel treated it with indifference. Why?

The next day Major Gibson dashed into camp and headed straight for his superior's canvassed shelter.

Pandemonium followed.

Officers ran back and forth, shouting conflicting orders. Breastworks were thrown up around the camp. A courier was dispatched to General Jackson at Fayetteville.

Jackson acted quickly.

By forced march he brought his militia and foot volunteers into camp within five hours.

It was from Gibson's scouts; Davy would piece together exactly what happened that day:

"Major Gibson hadn't yet returned, and we all began to think that he had been kill'd; and that night they put out a double guard. The next day the major got in, and brought a worse tale than I had, though he stated the same facts so far as I went. This seemed to put our colonel all in a fidget; and it convinced me, clearly, of one of the hateful ways of the world. When I made my report, I wasn't believed, because I was no officer; I was no great man, but just a poor soldier: But when Major Gibson reported the same thing! Why, then it was as true as preaching, and the colonel believed it every word."

Jackson's army entered camp emotionally, though not physically, ready to do battle. The long, coercive, march had taken its toll on their stomachs.

They were hungry, and hunger leads to bodily apathy.

Feeding 2,500 active soldiers required several hundred bushels of grain, tons of meat, gallons of whiskey, plus other provisions on a weekly basis. Supplies had been arriving sporadically and only in small quantities since beginning hostilities.

At 6′ 1″ and weighing in the neighborhood of 135 lbs, Jackson personally felt little need for food. Yet he had always empathized with the necessities of his command and wrote several furious letters to Washington.

He received no response.

One short portion of a Jackson letter has been credited to sundry leaders since:

> **Might I remind you, sirs, that an army marches on its stomach.**

This is when Davy Crockett became widely recognized among the volunteers from Tennessee.

To keep alive their waning spirits he told tales of his adventures as a boy over the eastern mountains, picturing the odd sorts who visited his father's tavern. He mimicked the old Dutchman who tried to make him his "little lad," and some of the wagoners he had known. He told of his adventures in hunting, and of "raslin' " bears. Whenever he lacked old stories, he invented new ones — both strange and comical — to keep his listeners in stitches.

Davy gained a reputation for "being the best fellow in the army." With his jokes, "fiddlin' " and generosity [2], his name echoed about the camp. "Know'd Davy Crockett? Why, ever'body know'd Davy!" a misty-eyed veteran of the Creek War recalled affectionately in 1856.

General Jackson tread packed dirt in front of his friend, Colonel Coffee; his tall gaunt frame, topped with a long yellow face and red-colored hair turning gray, frightening. He was sick, short-tempered, and suffering from a recent duel wound to his left shoulder, his arm still in a sling.

Coffee sat at his makeshift desk, nervously arranging papers.

Suddenly Jackson slammed his good fist on the desk, wincing from the pain it caused his left side. Papers flew everywhere.

"To hell with Washington! To hell with the provisions!" he bellowed.

Coffee jumped to attention.

"Gather your best mounted riflemen," he ordered. "I want to know just where those damn savages are! You'll lead them, Colonel. Take that man Crockett as your scout. Give him the rank of sergeant. Scour the whole countryside if you have to. We'll meet you at Ten Islands."

Coffee saluted, preparing to leave the tent.

"Oh, and John," said Jackson in a lower tone. "Tell the

men they'll have to fend for themselves for food. They're woodsmen. They can do it."

Within the hour, Coffee and his men galloped toward the Tennessee River. Two hours later, Jackson's main army headed for Ten Islands on the Coosa River.

Eight hundred volunteers crossed the Tennessee River to a settlement called Huntsville, moving northwest to Muscle Shoals, where they forded on to enemy ground.

Near the Black Warrior River, about one hundred miles south, they entered a Creek village apparently abandoned in haste for the Indians had left behind food supplies of corn and dried beans. These were confiscated and the village reduced to ashes.

They moved closer to the Ten Islands of the Coosa, an assemblage of ten green isles lying in the river. No Creeks were in sight, but Jackson's welcomed force could be seen in the distance.

General Jackson had just arrived, and his soldiers — on half rations and weak from hunger bordering on famish — were busily constructing a fort.

Colonel Coffee's appearance was as much welcomed as Jackson's had been less than fifteen minutes earlier. Davy Crockett was especially cheered. There would be stories tonight. True or not, no one cared.

Coffee, learning that he was now "General" Coffee, presented his report.

Jackson shook his head, told his friend to get some rest, and went to his maps.

"Those damn savages have to be around here somewhere," he rasped.

The next day Davy and George Russell were sent on a scouting mission.

"Find those damn savages!" had been the order.

"Where are the hostile Creeks?" asked Russell as they rode out of camp.

Davy shrugged and grinned.

Within four hours, the answer was in.

A large party of Creek warriors was hold up in a village less than nine miles away.

Jackson characteristically acted immediately.

Colonel Newton Cannon, replacing General Coffee, was dispatched with five hundred volunteers, with Davy positioned as lead scout.

Their objective: Destroy the village. Take prisoners, if possible.

Upon reaching the village, Cannon gave orders to surround it for a silent attack. Captain Zeb Hammond, with his company of rangers, would approach from the front.

Slowly, they moved in for the assault.
Suddenly, a loud yelp pierced the air.
They were spotted.

Clamoring to meet their enemy, the Indians had pressed Hammond back until he was shoulder to shoulder with the encompassing troops.

From all sides, the volunteers then began to close in on the desperate Red Sticks.

Hammond and his men, their courage renewed, started forward.

Volleys were fired. Red bodies fell en masse. Those left standing were taken prisoner.

Forty-six warriors were counted running into a long storage house centered in the village.

Cannon directed an attack on the wooden structure.

Advancing warily, arrows sailing from windows, they noticed an old squaw sitting in the doorway.

What was she doing?

They soon knew.

Using her feet against a bow for leverage, she pulled back the string and let fly an arrow that passed through the body of Lieutenant Richard "Dick" Moore, killing him instantly.

Incensed, the volunteers riddled the woman and torched the building.

All 46 warriors — plus — were burned alive.

One Indian, a little girl, managed to burst free of the inflamed housing; her hair and clothing ablaze, her burning arms beseechingly outstretched, she ran toward the line of volunteers. What she was doing there, no one knew or cared. A bullet cut short her soundless agony.

They then proceeded to slaughter the 186 braves held captive. Eighty-four women and children were bound and hustled away.

Davy felt sickened by the carnage. Earlier in the fighting, he had clubbed one of the volunteers for shooting an old Indian in the head.

"What'd ya do that fir, Davy?" asked the confused man, sitting dazed on the ground.

"We're here t' fight warriors! Not helpless ol' men!"

"Wal, he wuz an Injun, wuzn't he?" said the man, rubbing his temple. " 'sides, I want t' tell th' folks when I git home that I person'lly kilt me an Injun."

This battle, called the Battle of Tallushatchee, was one of degradation to civilized men.

But who's to judge? The volunteers were near starvation, tired, insane with passion. Many had lost kin at Fort Mims. Who's to judge sense in any battle? Or in any war?

An interesting footnote to the Battle of Tallushatchee gives us light into Andrew Jackson's inconsistent temperament.

He could be cruel and unforgiving, yet kind and protective.

While surveying the bloody battlefield, Davy spotted a dead squaw still clutching her living infant. Gently loosening her grasp, he picked the baby up and brought it back to camp, handing it to an astounded Jackson.

The general asked some of the Indian women to take the child and give him nourishment.

They refused.

"No!" they shook their heads in unison. "Kill him, too! All his relations are dead!"

Angrily dismissing the women, Jackson took the little one to his own tent, where he dissolved brown sugar in water and coaxed the boy into drinking. As much an orphan as he had once been, the infant's skin began to blend with his own.

Given the name Lincoya, the boy was taken to Huntsville for nursing, clothing and housing at Jackson's expense. Later he was sent to Jackson's plantation, The Hermitage, where Rachel Jackson accepted him into the family.

Unfortunately, Lincoya lived only fifteen years. When he died of tuberculosis on June 1, 1828, presidential candidate Jackson sadly said, "My son's early death was preordained from birth."

Fort Mims had been avenged. On November 9, 1813, the hostile Creeks attempted retaliation with an attack on a community of 154 friendly Creeks known as Fort Talladega, however the 1,100 enraged warriors led by Red Eagle himself were routed by Jackson's 2,000 volunteers.

The battles raged on through winter. In it's midst the cold, hungry volunteers began to desert. Davy — leading 799 Tennesseans — trotted his horse across a bridge from the fort, past a cannon "with a lighted match to destroy them [3]" and rode home.

His enlistment was over.

He would not rejoin Jackson's forces until September 18, 1814.

Old Hickory, left with a handful of men and an indomitable will of a commander, continued to wear the Creeks down.

Jackson hoped to windup this sidetracking little conflict by the end of March.

On January 14th, seven hundred and ninety-nine volunteers entered camp unannounced.

"Sergeant Crockett sends his greetings, General," said George Russell, dismounting and forming the proper salute.

Then, on February 6th, the 39th Regimental Infantry arrived.

Throughout February, food supplies and provisions were brought in.

By mid-March, Jackson's army had grown to nearly five thousand strong.

On March 14, 1814, the campaign to obliterate Weatherford's Red Sticks and culminate the Creek War began.

Leaving a contingent of 450 to guard the newly built fort, Jackson and his army rode southward along the Coosa River, then eastward to Horseshoe Bend.

Horseshoe Bend, on the Tallapoosa River, was a 100-acre wooded peninsula surrounded three-quarters by water. The Indian's had fortified it against attack with a five to eight foot high breastwork running across its 350-yard neck. Portholes were arranged so "a force approaching it would be exposed to double fire, while they lay in perfect security behind [4]." One thousand hostiles, gathered from the villages of Oakuskee, Oakchays, New Youka, Hillabees, the Fish Pond and Eufala, silently awaited Jackson's arrival. Menewa, a half-breed known as Chief Great Warrior, was in charge of the defense.

When Jackson reached the Bend on March 27th, he was amazed. "It is difficult to conceive," he wrote in his report, "a situation more eligible for defense than the one they had chosen, or one rendered more secure by the skill with which they erected their breastworks."

Several hours earlier he had detailed General Coffee, with his "mounted gunmen," across the river to block escape by fleeing Red Sticks.

Coffee, too, was to create a diversion in order to draw the enemy's attention from the principal point of attack — the protective breastwork.

Jackson positioned his artillery on a small hill, stationing one 6-pounder and one 3-pounder at appropriate distances from the formidable fortress. At 10:30 a.m. he opened fire, the balls striking with no effect. For two hours, cannon blasted the stronghold without significance.

Coffee, meanwhile, had loosed the Creek canoes from their moorings and was using them to ferry his soldiers and Indian allies for an assault to the rear of the encampment.

Setting fire to a cluster of huts near the Bend, Coffee and his men stealthily worked their way around the yard.

As smoke billowed from the burning huts, Jackson directed his men to storm the breastworks.

Under an onslaught of rifles and arrows, the 39th Infantry charged forward.

Reaching the rampart, they thrust their weapons through the portholes and fired at the stunned and frightened Indians backing for the thick brush covering the grounds. Major Lemuel P. Montgomery — descended from American General Richard Montgomery, who fell early in the Battle of Quebec in 1775 — leaped on the wall, calling for his men to follow. A musket ball struck him in the head, sending him sprawling lifeless.

Lt. Sam Houston took up the cry and scaled the wall.

An arrow shattered a leg but he jumped inside the compound, bolstered by the shouting regulars.

Total bloodshed ensued. Red Sticks were shot down as they hid behind bushes. Others made for their canoes, only to run into Coffee. Still others tried concealment beneath fallen trees.

Throughout the afternoon, it continued. The Indians were flushed from hiding places and shot as they frantically sought new cover.

The Red Sticks were now entirely disassembled. They scampered in utter disarray, screaming as tiny missiles tore flesh.

Only darkness saved the few who managed to escape.

Still, all was not finished. Sixteen hostiles were found hiding "under the banks" the next morning, and unceremoniously slain.

A stringent count following the battle showed 557 dead hostiles on the battlefield itself, with 300 drowned or shot trying to escape across the river. Of the Americans, 49 were dead and 159 wounded. General Coffee's Creek and Cherokee allies numbered 23 dead and 47 wounded. Captives totaled 300 (four men, and 296 women and children).

For an exact calculation of the hostile dead, Jackson had ordered his men to slice off the nose tip of each Red Stick counted. Coffee's Indian allies scalped their portion of the count.

It was later questioned anonymously: "The Indian scalps his dead enemy, while we cut off the tip of the nose. Are we any less savage?"

General Andrew Jackson was inimitably victorious, yet not entirely happy. Neither Red Eagle nor his underling, Menewa, were among the dead or captured. They had slipped his assiduous grasp.

"Damn tricky savages," he muttered.

The Battle of Horseshoe Bend literally crushed the hostile Creeks' will and capacity to wage further war.

Ironically, as the battle raged, British troops prepared to land at Pensacola — off the Gulf of Mexico — with an abundant supply of arms and ammunition for Indian use. Had the encounter been delayed, history would have taken a different course.

On the afternoon of March 28th, astride his huge white stallion, Jackson addressed his army in a clear, resonant voice.

"Soldiers," he began. "You have entitled yourselves to the gratitude of your country and your general. The expedition, from which you have just returned, has, by your good conduct, been rendered prosperous beyond any example in the history of warfare. It has redeemed the character of state, and of that description of troops of which the greater part of you are.

"You have, within a few days, opened your way to the Tallapoosie [sic], and destroyed a confederacy of the enemy, furious by nature, and grown insolent from impunity. Relying on their numbers, the security of their situation, and the assurances of their prophets, they derided our approach, and already exalted in the victory they expected to obtain. But they were ignorant of the influence of government on the human powers, nor knew what brave men, and civilized, could effect. By their yells, they hoped to frighten us, and with their wooden fortifications to oppose us. Stupid mortals! Their yells but designated their situation the more certainly; while their walls became a snare for their own destructions.

"So will it ever be when presumption and ignorance contend against bravery and prudence.

"The fiends of the Tallapoosie will no longer murder our women and children, or disturb the quiet of our borders. Their midnight flambeaux will no longer illumine their council-house, or shine upon the victim of their infernal orgies. In their places, a new generation will arise who know their duty better. The weapons of warfare will be exchanged for utensils of husbandry; and the wilderness, which now withers in sterility, and mourns the desolation which overspreads her, will blossom as a rose, and become the nursery of the arts. But before this happy day can arrive, other chastisements remain to be inflicted. It is indeed lamentable that the path to peace should lead through blood, and over the bodies of the slain; but it is a dispensation of Providence to inflict partial evils, that good may be produced.

"Our enemies are not sufficiently humbled; they do not sue for peace. A collection of them awaits our approach, and remains to be dispersed.

"Buried in ignorance, and seduced by their prophets, they have the weakness to believe they will be able to make a stand against us. The hopes, which have so long deluded them, must be driven from their last refuge. They must be made to know that their prophets are impostors, and that our strength is mighty, and will prevail. Then, and not till then, may we expect to make with them a peace that will be lasting."

On April 5, 1814, the army set out for the Holy Grounds [5], coupling the Coosa and Tallapoosa Rivers, torching Indian villages along the way.

On April 18th, Jackson initiated construction of a fort over the site of old French Fort Toulouse — once used by the Indians — near Wetumpka, Alabama. It was renamed Fort Jackson in his honor.

In August, against his superiors' wishes because of his harsh judgment toward the red man collectively, Jackson held peace negotiations with the assembled chiefs of the Creek Nation in a tent on the grounds of Fort Jackson.

Red Eagle, his indignation fettered, looked into the face of the man they now called "Sharp Knife." He saw no sympathy for the vanquished.

"For your crimes," Jackson told them, his face hardened to stone, "you must pay the United States government 23 million acres of land. You must give us three-fifths of Alabama, and one-fifth of Georgia. In addition, you must cease all communications with the British and Spanish. You must acknowledge the United States' right to open roads through your land in order to establish military and trading posts wherever we deem it necessary. And you must surrender to us all instigators of this past war."

Jackson's words were translated through an interpreter named George Mayfield. Mayfield, stolen as a child in a Creek raid and raised as one of their own, believed the general's terms too harsh and unjust, but kept these feelings to himself that afternoon.

The chiefs craved and were granted private council to discuss the imposed conditions.

The following day, Mayfield interpreted the words of an enormous Creek who stepped forward to plead the Indian cause. Big Warrior, never hostile to white men, had spoken to Mayfield in council the previous night and had come to "Sharp Knife" with a masterly oration:

"Many Creeks and Cherokees have allied with the white man against their own people in a war you call the Creek War. I have also done so, that the treaty made by the Creeks long ago with Father Washington might not be broken.

"To his friendly arm I hold fast. I will never break the chain of friendship we made together. He was father to all people under the sun!

(Big Warrior held out the treaty signed by George Washington.)

"His talk I now hold in my hand."

Jackson stared impassive.

"Our people admit," the chief continued, "that the American claim to indemnity is just. We are willing, as friends of the United States to give up part of our land; but our habits are not always the habits of the white man. We hunt on this land, as did our ancestors before us. Our hunting grounds must be large for us to survive. We therefore ask that you leave us in possession of the rich lands west of the Coosa River."

Jackson eyed the big chief for a moment, then motioned him to sit with the others. All Indians — friendly or hostile — must be dealt with equally.

Clearing his throat, he formed words carefully so as not to have them misinterpreted:

"You [the Creek Nation] must be cut off from the mischiefmakers from the Lakes. Until this is done your nation cannot expect happiness, nor mine security. Therefore, your request is denied. We will, however, guarantee you the right to own forever the land remaining to you.

"This evening must determine whether or not you are disposed to becoming friendly. Rejecting the treaty will show you to be the enemies of the United States… And mark my creed, should we again be provoked. 'An eye for an eye, toothe for toothe [sic], scalp for scalp.' "

The chiefs once more withdrew to council.

At 2 p.m. on August 9, 1814, thirty-five chiefs, of whom only Red Eagle was hostile, signed the treaty under protest. Before their marks were dry, each departed to carry tidings of disgrace to their tribe.

Jackson's promise that the Creeks could "own forever the land remaining" to them was not kept.

When they ceded their territory to the United States, they laid open a procedure by which five southeastern tribes — Creeks, Cherokees, Chickasaws, Choctaws, Seminoles — were systematically removed from their ancestral estates and pushed westward. Crockett attempted a cessation of the

"Indian Removal Bill" when a congressman during Jackson's administration, arguing: "The United States should honor treaties made with the tribes."

His protests, unfortunately, fell on deaf ears. Congress passed it in 1830, sweeping it along for President Jackson's flourished signature.

The Creek War had officially ended.

But the War of 1812 continued.

On August 24, 1814, British forces under the joint command of General Robert Ross and Admiral George Cockburn invaded Washington City, burning the president's mansion and the capital.

Three days earlier, General Jackson had received reports of a massive British build-up in the Gulf of Mexico. While President James Madison and his cabinet anxiously awaited news from Chesapeake that the enemy had been repelled, Jackson and his army were en route to the Spanish city of Pensacola in western Florida.

Some accounts place Davy Crockett with Jackson during his Pensacola campaign against the British. Did he also fight alongside Old Hickory in the victorious Battle of New Orleans?

Davy himself claimed otherwise:

"After peace was made with the body of the [Indian] nation, I scouted a little for hostiles who were holding out, but, not finding any, I went home. This closed my career as a warrior. I never liked this business with the Indians. I was glad to be through with these war matters. They had no fun in them at all. It was nothing but dog eat dog."

Davy's own account appears the more plausible. He was a scout and backwoods fighter. Not disciplined for British warfare.

True military fame would not be his until March 6, 1836.

Part Two

Sadness, Politics…and Congress

Chapter 5

Davy rode home in April of 1815. He felt no need to tell his family where he had been between December of 1813 and his return to active duty on September 18, 1814. They thought he was at war. Why not allow them to continue thinking that? He simply needed time alone.

Polly was busy scrubbing little Willie's shirt, which never seemed to come clean. The children were playing a game of "Hide-And-Go-Seek."

They had grown some. John Wesley was 8. Willie, 4. And little Margaret, whom Davy would call "Li'l Polly," toddled along at the age of 3.

"Hullo, th' house. I'm home," yelled Davy, dismounting his weary horse.

"Who goes there, stranger?" yelled back Polly, holding Willie's tattered shirt at arms length and shaking her head in dismay.

"Why, it's paw!" shouted the children, racing to grasp their dad. All except Margaret, who turned so sharply she fell on her little behind.

"Do I know you, stranger?" teased Polly, scooping up Margaret and placing her in her father's arms.

"Ya will t'night," chuckled Davy.

Within a week, they were again in the bear rug business. And the money, almost nonexistent for the past three years, provided the children with "store bought" clothes and Polly with a "store bought" dress.

Then death, "that cruel leveler of distinction," struck.

Polly fainted while mending a hole in one of the bear-skins.

Overburdened with farm work, with malaria contracted as a youth still coursing through her veins, her constitution suffered during Davy's absence. By the time of his return, her heart was beginning to fail.

Davy carried her into the cabin and laid her gently on the bed. The two boys covered her with blankets. Margaret crawled beneath the blankets and put her tiny arms around her mother's neck. Polly stirred, then choked. She couldn't breathe. Quickly, Davy removed his daughter and unbut-toned the top of his wife's dress. The choking stopped, but she was burning with fever. She lapsed again into uncon-sciousness. Davy ran for a bucket of cool spring water and, dousing a cloth and nervously wringing it out, patted damp-ness from her inflamed brow as unchecked tears mixed with his own perspiration.

Laying the cloth tenderly on her forehead, he sat dolefully by the bed. Waiting for her to awaken.

She never regained consciousness, slipping into oblivion at the age of 27.

He buried her in the forest next to the farm. Over her grave he formed a cairn of limestone boulders.

Three figures stood by this gravesite in a declining light. The two sons and Davy, with "Li'l Polly" nestled in his arms.

Heartbroken and sick with guilt, he gave up any thought of continuing in the bear rug business and wandered into the greening forest, leaving the children in the trusted care of his married brother.

Deeper and deeper he strayed, further and further into the Tennessee wilderness.

Caring little for his own safety as beasts growled, he walked his horse over pine-strewn paths, paying them no mind. If he died between the salivating jaws of a bear or panther, it mattered naught. He would rejoin his lost love. A love he should never have left alone to such a menacing country.

Eating little, sleeping less, he drifted high to a mountain overlooking a world he knew. A world his Polly would never again see.

Then slowly, mechanically, he turned and retraced his steps toward home and family. To the children, she had been an affectionate mother. To him, a loving wife. This he would never forget. For love is never lost, as long as it stays remembered.

Elizabeth Margaret Patton was lonely.

Born on May 22, 1788 to a prosperous farmer, she married her first cousin and moved from North Carolina to Franklin County, Tennessee around 1812. Within two years James Patton was dead, a casualty of the Creek War, leaving his young widow to support two small children and a 200-acre farm not far from Davy's sparse piece of land.

Trotting homeward, Davy noticed a young woman hanging wash. Two children, a boy and a girl, were sitting on the ground beside her.

She was a large woman. Hardly one considered beautiful or even pretty. Yet her features were handsome in a feminine way, her smile beguiling as she tickled the youngsters with her foot.

"Oh well," he must have thought, prompting his horse into a gallop.

Still, the memory of that smile remained.

On May 22, 1816, in celebration of her birthday, Davy took Elizabeth's hand in marriage. In attendance were well wishing friends and relatives representing both families.

"Polly would have been proud," he later wrote.

Thus began Davy Crockett's most affluent union.

As the spousal owner of 200-acres of prime land he was elected a lieutenant in Franklin County's militia, which led to an offer to run for the state's legislature.

This he refused, laughing, "Speech-makin' makes m' knees feel mighty weak."

In 1817, the Crockett's leased two adjacent farmlands and moved to Shoal Creek, Lawrence County.

Here, they built a small business empire.

Erecting a water-powered gristmill on the one farm, corn was turned into cornmeal. Around fourteen bushels of meal were produced each day, with the average sold around ten bushels. Surplus was sent to Davy's distillery, constructed on the adjoining farm, where employees mixed it with water and allowed it to ferment. Later, a wood-kindled still converted the mash into whiskey.

By the end of 1817, they also established a gunpowder factory. More than seven thousand pounds of powder was manufactured a year at 37¢ per pound.

Businessman Crockett was doing well, powered by his efficient managerial guide — Elizabeth Patton Crockett.

In 1818, settlers poured into Shoal Creek on a daily basis.

Its community was growing.

And, along with the good, came ruffians and thieves.

As no law had yet been established in this new land, the peaceful were understandably frightened. Many were often beaten and robbed of their possessions

Deciding to halt the violence, residents secretly gathered to commission constables for arrests and a judge to administer punishment.

Several settlers volunteered to enforce the law, though none felt qualified to discipline the outlaws.

"What 'bout that man, Crockett?" declared one of the new constables. "From what I hear'd he's got natur'l born sense. Why, he don't even need t' shoot game if'n he don't care t'. He cin jist look a critter in th' eye an' they'll holler, 'Don't shoot, Davy! I'll come peace'ble!"

So it was that Davy Crockett became magistrate of Shoal Creek.

"This will be hard bus'ness fir me," he told Elizabeth when he heard the news. I cin jist barely write m' own name so's people cin read it."

Court was held in a cabin adjacent to the whiskey distillery.

No warrants were issued.

The constables were simply told to "Catch those varmints an' bring 'em in fir trial." Some came in alive; publicly whipped for their misdeeds, then sent crawling back to wherever they called home. Others came in slung over a saddle, given a mock trial, and buried. Those beaten "resistin' arrest" were released with a promise to leave the country, never to return.

"I wish t' be shot," grinned Davy, handing a bruised culprit a swig of whiskey, "if'n I ever see yir face 'round these parts, agin. An yir'll be shot if'n I do."

According to descendants in Lawrence County, Tennessee, none of the banished outlaws ever returned.

Still, however pleased the settlers of Shoal Creek were in Davy's handling of the criminal element, the Tennessee State Legislature was not.

On November 3, 1818 they enacted a law, directed inclusively toward Magistrate Crockett, requiring all legal matters in writing:

"Warrants have to be issued, and all records of proceedings kept."

Taking this in stride, Davy read whatever books on law available and practiced the art of handwriting.

Thereafter, no offender was brought in without a warrant and no judgment bestowed without an official report.

Bottoming every document was fixed the words: "Be always sure your right, then go ahead." A motto ascribed him for the rest on his life.

Although law and order had been established in Shoal Creek itself, bands of brigands still roamed the countryside. Nerves were again on edge in 1820. To quash any potential carnage, settlers formed the 57th Regimental Militia, with Davy Crockett appointed to strike the outlaws in their own lairs.

As Lieutenant Colonel Crockett, Davy personally led his militia to victory in each raid, tearing into the threatening bandits with such force they had no alternative but to surrender — or to die where they stood.

Those who surrendered were hauled back to court, whipped by the colonel himself, then jailed for terms appropriating their crimes.

Warrants and records were officially filed.

In 1821, Davy was asked again to run for the Tennessee State Legislature.

This time he accepted.

His opponent was a fat-jowled, boorish lawmaker named L. Phineas Hogan, who loved whiskey, money and easy living. Though relishing votes, he hated voters.

"Country bumpkins," he scowled, raising a toddy to his ample lips, his meek-looking secretary scrambling to wipe spills from his employer's shirtfront.

"And Crockett!" he growled, pushing the young man out of the way. "I won't have any trouble defeating that ignorant bear hunter. He doesn't know a tariff from a turnip, I'll wager."

With this last remark, Hogan doubled with laughter, his drink splashing. Cursing, he jumped from his chair as hot liquid burned through his shirting.

"Hogan!" came a voice beneath his hotel window.

"Well, see who it is!" he screamed, gingerly examining the glowing blotch on his stomach.

"There's a group of backwoodsmen out here, sir," said the secretary, pulling in his head from the window. "They want to see you."

Hogan, lambasting every inconvenience known to mankind, stepped onto the balcony and stared with distaste. About twenty men smilingly gazed up at him. At their head was a buckskin-clad hunter he recognized, a long rifle resting in the crook of one arm.

"What do you want with me, Crockett? You'd best be out trying to get votes. You'll need them."

"Wal," grinned Davy, "that's what we come t' see ya fir, Hogan. Some of us Duck River boys are goin' on a squirrel hunt. We're goin' t' be out two days an' then have us a big barb'cue. Th' boys think we ought t' make a political hunt of it."

"What does that mean?" asked Hogan suspiciously.

"Ya round up some of yir men an' th' side that shows up with th' fewest squirrel scalps has t' pay fir th' whole frolic."

The portly politician frowned. The thought of tramping through the wilderness in hot June weather, or in any kind of weather for that matter, was not to his liking.

"You'll find politics is something different from a squirrel hunt, Crockett," he barked. "Why don't you stick to your 'b'ar huntin',' and leave government to men who know something about it."

Grumbling protests rose from below.

" 'fraid you'll have t' buy somebody a drink, Hogan?" yelled one.

"A li'l exercise'll take some o' that blubber off'n yir sides," bawled another.

"We think a heap more o' bein' a good sport than we do o' oratory," chided a third.

"All right," snorted Hogan, raising both hands to quiet the din. "I accept you're wager. I'll show you I can round up squirrel hunters as well as voters, **Mister** Crockett!"

Two days later, two hunting parties entered Shoal Creek's

excited settlement. Davy Crockett led one, with his usual grin and wave.

The other was followed — rather than led — by a bloated, puffing lump in dirty buckskins. He was hatless, his gray hair matted and sticking out in every direction, his face a mask of mud. Painfully, he limped toward the stump that was to represent his oratorical victory and sat down heavily, nearly missing his intended seat. His own men joined in the roar of laughter.

"Ya met me on m' own ground, Hogan," said Davy, quieting the uncontrollable merriment at his opponent's expense. "What's yir tally?"

"A hundred and twenty-six," answered a rifleman for the speechless Hogan, reaching into a buckskin sack for the skins.

"We'll take yir word fir it," chuckled Davy. "We got two hundred an' fifty-one. I guess that means our friend Hogan pays fir th' shindig."

Lifting a tired arm weakly in agreement, Hogan pitched face first to the soft grass.

More peels of laughter.

Davy won the election 2-to-1. Voters, as people, never forget humiliation.

Shortly following the election, Davy met Colonel James K. Polk [1] at a dinner held in Pulaski, Tennessee. What could have been an embarrassing situation, surfaced as a comical recollection:

"He was at that time a member elected to the legislature,

as well as myself; and in a large company he said to me, 'Well, colonel, I suppose we shall have a radical change of the judiciary at the next session of the legislature.' 'Very likely, sir,' says I; and I put out quickly, for I was afraid someone would ask me what the judiciary was, and if I know'd I wish to be shot. I don't indeed believe I had ever before heard that there was any such thing in all nature; but still I was not willing that the people there should know how ignorant I was about it."

Although Davy admittedly knew "li'l 'bout gov'rment," he knew right from wrong.

When the Tennessee State Legislature met at Murfreesboro — then the capital of Tennessee — in September, his first act was to defend the rights of poor farmers in danger of losing their lands.

The problem stemmed from warrants issued during the Revolutionary War by North Carolina, of which Tennessee was then a part. These warrants now gave veterans authorization to claim Tennessee lands already worked by farmers, forcing them to leave their homes of many years. Davy's arguments managed to curb this practice, but were unable to bring it to a standstill.

While Davy fought for the plight of his constituents, he was on the verge himself of going bankrupt.

Heavy rains had caused the stream upon which he had built his gristmill, distillery and gunpowder factory to overflow its banks, sweeping away the entire business.

When he rode home to inspect the damage, he found Elizabeth and the children safe but the grounds on which his enterprises once stood were torn, empty spaces.

"They [the businesses] had cost me upwards of three thousand dollars," wrote Davy. "The first news when I got to the legislature was that my mills were — not blown up sky high, as you would guess, by my powder establishment — but swept away all to smash by a large freshet, that came soon after I left home…"

Davy, having borrowed heavily to complete the businesses, was now in considerable debt.

Sadly shaking his head, he looked at Elizabeth and the children. Elizabeth grabbed his hand and smiled. It brought back the day he had first seen her following the death of Polly. It gave him the strength to go on then…

"Just pay up, Davy," she squeezed his hand. "We'll sell everything to pay our debts, then everybody will be happy and we'll scuffle for more."

"This was just such talk as I wanted to hear," Davy recalled in his autobiography, "for a man's wife can hold him devilish uneasy, if she begins to scold and fret, and perplex him, at a time he has a full load for a railroad car on his mind already.

"And so, you see, I determined not to break full handed, but thought it better to keep a good conscious with an empty purse, than to get a bad opinion of myself, with a full one. I therefore gave up all I had, and took on a bran-fire new start."

Situated in western Tennessee near the Mississippi River is a land still known today as the Shakes.

In the year 1811, a devastating earthquake uprooted several thousand aged trees, opening fissures and splitting the loose earth into separate banks. Water flowed into these cracks, creating the rivers of Forked Deer, Hatchee, Reelfoot and Obion, all converging into the Mississippi.

It was on the banks of the Obion River that Davy chose to resettle his family.

Aftershocks of the great quake were felt for a year as far north as Canada, to the east as far as Boston, and southward to New Orleans. As late as 1822, small tremblers disrupted the region.

One day, Davy's cap shook from his head as he planted corn.

Sitting on a stump, he gathered his startled family to him and told of an Indian legend:

" 'Fore th' earthquake there liv'd on these banks an ol' Chickasaw chief whose son had a clubfoot. Since th' foot made him reel as he walk'd, he was call'd Reelfoot. When this unhappy lad grew t' manhood he wander'd t' th' land o' th' Choctaws, where he met an' fell in love with a beau-t'ful Indian maiden. He wanted t' marry her, but her father refus'd t' give his daughter t' a man with a clubfoot. So Reelfoot stole her away t' be his bride. When he discover'd this th' Choctaw chief, her father, put a curse on Reelfoot an' all his tribe, prophesyin' that th' Great Spirit would stomp upon their land an' destroy it."

"So let that be a lesson t' ya," Davy instructed the boys, playfully jostling the youngest. "Never steal a gal her paw don't want ya t' have."

Suddenly, 15-year-old John Wesley sprang to the stump and wrestled his pa to the ground. The other boys and girls leaped to the fray, tickling the 6′ 3″ backwoodsman until all strength left him. Elizabeth, removing a moccasin, tickled his bare foot until Davy — who boasted to never giving up on anything — gave up.

In May of 1822, Davy's political supporters awarded him a .41-caliber, side-locked percussion Kentucky rifle, crafted by John M. Graham of Pennsylvania. It's inscription simply read: "Presented to David Crockett at Nashville, Tenn., May 5, 1822."

Affectionately rubbing its fine-grained stock, he whispered for none to hear.

"Ol' Betsy."

His pet name for Elizabeth.

In the latter part of May, he held out Ol'Betsy to Elizabeth.

"Presented to **David** Crockett at Nashville, Tenn., May 5, 1822," he read, as he had read each day since receiving it. "I've been call'd **Davy** since I wuz a boy, Betsy. Perhaps I should call m'self **David** now that I'm grown up an' in politics. But you cin still call me **Davy**."

Elizabeth agreed to the change for everyone except her.

In July of 1822, now Representative **David** Crockett, he was back at Murfreesboro.

Again he fought the hated land warrants, while championing a bill to aid widows and children.

When a bill to outlaw gambling in the state came up for a vote, he opposed it with a vengeance. "Freedom," he argued, "is bein' taken away on all sides. I see no harm in bettin' on cards, horse's, or shootin' matches."

David Crockett served two terms in the Tennessee State Legislature.

In 1825, he ran for Congress, though telling Elizabeth apprehensively: "It's a step above my knowledge. I know nothin' 'about matters in Congress."

Still, he felt obliged to take the plunge. Perhaps, he even thought, it would lead him to the presidency.

"President Crockett," he danced Elizabeth around. "Now wouldn't that be a kick."

His opponent was surveyor, planter and at-large politician Adam Rankin Alexander, who had voted for Secretary of State Henry Clay's bill for higher tariffs.

David was confident Alexander would lose on this issue alone, since high tariffs meant higher prices for imported goods.

Unfortunately, times were good for the state's main industry that year. Cotton sold for $25 per hundredweight and Alexander would credit the new tariff law, emphasizing: "If it raised the price of cotton, it will raise the price of everything you grow or make to sell."

As unpopular as he had been in the past, voters turned their capricious heads toward Alexander.

David lost the election that August, drawing 2,599 votes to Alexander's 2,866.

"I might as well have sung psalms over a dead horse, as to try to make th' people believe otherwise," he recalled later to a friend, "for they know'd their cotton had raised, sure enough, an' if th' con'l [Alexander] hadn't done it, they didn't know what had."

Back home at the Shakes, David struck on a new business idea.

During his campaigning he heard that narrow strips of wood used in making barrels, called staves, were in considerable demand in New Orleans.

Politics, he decided, would have to be placed on a back burner. Untold riches awaited him.

Contracting to supply around 30,000, he hired men to cut the staves, as others built two flatboats to waft them to market.

In January of 1826, David Crockett — with a crew of inexperienced riverboat men and a pilot — floated smoothly down the Obion to the Mississippi.

The Big Old Strong River, as the Indians respectfully called it, opened wide and treacherous. Churning white waters met the incoming barges, threatening to whirl them with an overwhelming force and smash them asunder. The oarsmen fought with Herculean strength but sawyers, loosed by the long-ago earthquake, snagged the bladed levers as a swift current trembled the heavy loads.

David ordered the boats lashed together. This was a mistake, for the crew found they were unable to keep the flatboats straight. So down the river they went, helplessly coursing sideways.

At last, the water grew calm.

Thinking the worst over, David slipped to the boat's cabin to ponder his position. The vessels needed righting. He would loose them and… Suddenly he heard running, shouting. The cabin swirled as if every oar was wrenched in a single direction.

As the cabin turned broadside, water poured in from the hatch. David looked around for an escape. The only way out was a small hatchway standing uppermost, a sliver of dark sky peeking. Thrusting his hands through the tiny opening, he roared for assistance.

"Pull," he shouted.

Two hefty boatmen grabbed his hands and arms. "Its neck or nothin', come out or sink." With an enormous heave they yanked him free, wood splintering as the little hole grew in size.

David and his weary crew were now perched topside of the overturned forward boat.

Then, without warning, it plunged downward.

"She's goin' under," yelled a crewman.

They scrambled to the rearward boat, still lashed to the forward, which stooped at a perilous angle. She, too, was being drawn beneath the quivery surface.

"Driftwood," cried another boatman, vaulting to his feet.

Trees and logs, gathered by the powerful current, formed a raft, which verged close enough to obtain by towrope. Assembling what remained of their strength, they fastened the rope to the floating platform and tugged themselves to safety.

"Wal, boys," said David, watching his fortune descend into the murky darkness. "If a man's born fir hangin', he need have no fear o' drownin'."

A few minutes later, he chuckled.

"What's funny, Da…huh, David?" asked a raveled crewman, checking his half-naked body for slivers.

"I wuz jist thinkin'," David shook his head in amusement. "When I git t' Congress, I'll pass a law preventin' fools from goin' int' th' wood stave bus'ness."

Stories of David "Davy" Crockett's latest adventure preceded him home.

"We hear'd you went straight down t' th' bottom o' th' river an' stay'd there when th' boat turn'd over," beamed Matilda, his youngest.

David bent to pick her up.

"Do tell."

"An' when you'd come up," the girl went on excitedly,

"you'd travel'd all over th' river bottom. A man said you wuzn't even wet when you come up. He said you could run faster, dive deeper, stay under longer, an' come up dryer than any man in creation."

Raising his giggling daughter above his head, he looked at Elizabeth.

"I reckon I 'peared a might cracklin' when they drugg'd me out o' that hatch-hole. But I wuzn't dry, I wuz wet all over. Where did that tale come from?"

"It's spread out all over the county, Davy. And they say you're going to run for Congress, again."

"I might," grinned David, enjoying Betsy's use of his old name. "I jist might."

In 1827, cotton prices deflated to $6 per hundredweight.

Farmers cursed Alexander, and Clay's high tariff. What they grew sold at low prices, yet supplies cost more than they could afford.

David knew incumbent Alexander would be an easy victory for sure this time. But two other candidates — William Arnold and John Cooke — soon entered to make it a four-way race.

However, Cooke had quit the campaign in disgust shortly following a heated confrontation with Crockett, leaving Alexander and Arnold to face the "ignorant bear hunter."

According to records found in Davidson County Courthouse, Nashville, Tennessee, Cooke had "gotten into it" with David during one of the latter's rallies.

Both had slurred each other's character since their first encounter that spring, and this meeting brought it to a head.

"Wal, who do we have here?" David bawled when he noticed his antagonist standing in the audience.

Cooke had decided to ridicule Crockett from the race that day, taking along a witness for backup.

"If it ain't Gen'l Cooke, one o' th' best storytellers in th' district. Even better'n m'self. Only m' stories 'bout m' worthy opponent are true as gospel, while his lies 'bout me are…"

Cooke was furious and charged the podium.

"You're nothing but a drunkard, a gambler and an adulterer," he shook a clenched fist, his knuckles dead white. "Only a fool would vote for such an immoral lout."

Bracing himself for a sudden attack by the big man, he planted his feet firmly on the ground.

Instead, David played the game by telling even greater lies about Cooke.

His face beet purple, Cooke turned to his witness.

"You know me, Will. Are those things this… this… Gentleman said about me true?

"No, they're not, John."

"See!" smiled Cooke smugly.

"Wal," David, delighting in the short return to his ***Davy*** image, shrugged and grinned to his animated listeners thoroughly enjoying the entertainment, "I guess that means both o' us are liars."

Two weeks later, dressed in his "Sunday best," David climbed to the rostrum and sat beside Adam Alexander and

William Arnold. He grinned and waved.

The crowd cheered.

"Seeing how you're so popular, Colonel Crockett," said Alexander. "Why don't you speak first? Let the people know what you think."

As David stood and walked to the rail squaring the podium, Alexander turned a sly wink toward Arnold. Crockett was a joke.

David gave a short, soft, homely talk inundated with witty anecdotes. Then returned to his seat.

Alexander spoke next — nearly lulling his listeners to sleep — for one hour and thirty-five minutes.

Arnold stepped up third.

Neither candidate had mentioned David Crockett.

About that time a flock of guinea hens wandered near the platform, chattering in their highest key. Arnold sputtered, stopped his haranguing of Alexander, and refused to continue until the fowls were removed.

"M'ybe they're tryin' t' tell ya somethin', Gen'l," offered David.

"Oh, shut up, Crockett!" shouted Arnold.

"At least he knows I'm here," David elbowed Alexander, who stared straight ahead.

An agitated Arnold sat down.

David stood up and grabbed his hand, declaring loud enough for everyone to hear:

"Well, Con'l [2], you're th' first man I ever saw that really understands th' language o' th' fowls. Ya never mentioned me at all in yir speech, though ya talk'd 'bout th' other feller badly enough. But when m' li'l friends, th'guinea fowls, came up, cryin' 'CR-CR-TT, CR-CR-TT,' ya drove 'em all away. Seems t' me that sounds an awful lot like 'CROCK-ETT, CROCK-ETT.' I guess they knows a good man when they sees'em."

And everyone held rib-tickled sides. Everyone, that is, except William Arnold and Adam Rankin Alexander.

David Crockett carried the day, and the election. When the polls were tallied, he was a new Congressman from Tennessee by more than 2, 000 votes.

Chapter 6

"Mr. Speaker, I cin outspeak any man on this floor an' give 'em two hours start. I cin outlook a panther, outstare a flash o' lightnin', tote a steamboat on m' back, an' play at rough an' tumble with a lion. I cin walk like an ox, run like fox, spout like a volcano, an' swallow a man whole if'n ya butter his head an' pin his ears back…"

So began David Crockett's first speech before the House of Representatives in October of 1827.

Washington City was in for a treat.

A curious freak to its sophisticated society, the "Canebrake Congressman" soon became its topic of conversation. Everywhere, he fed to its citizen's amusement.

"I'm David Crockett," he told an inquiring bevy surrounding him one day. "Fresh from th' backwoods, half-horse, half-alligator, a li'l touch o' snappn' turtle. I cin wade th' Mississippi, leap th' Ohio, ride a streak o' lightnin', slip without a scratch down a honey locust, whip m' weight in wildcats, hug a bear too close fir comfort, an' eat any man opposed t' Jackson."

Eastern newspaper printed every word, every sentence, every formal and informal discourse by the junior Congressman, placing emphasis on his loyalty to General Jackson.

Although David Crockett outwardly acted the fool, he was hardly that.

Andrew Jackson had lost his bid for the presidency in 1824 through a house vote for John Quincy Adams. In the three years since, Adams' popularity had diminished, while Jackson's had steadily grown. Congressman Crockett intended to be part of the winning faction in 1828.

But the year was still 1827.

After satisfying his claim as a Jackson supporter, David settled to work in the straightforward, no-nonsense manner notable during his legislative terms.

Jokes and "tomfoolery" became fewer. Speeches and arguments, ghostwritten by Whig Congressman Thomas Chilton of Kentucky, surprised even those who protested, "Crockett knows nothing of the rules of debate."

An old nemesis — the Tennessee land warrant grants — entered the House under a redesigned venality. They were now sold to speculators who laid claim to the best tracks in the district. Farmers were forced to barren or inaccessible lands in which the speculators had scorned or overlooked.

To add to this affliction, they were burdened with heavy

taxes to pay for an expensive survey of the region ordered by the speculators.

Unknown to Congressman Crockett at that time, Andrew Jackson was one of the speculators.

"I have seen," spoke David in the House, "the last blanket of an honest, industrious, poor family sold under the hammer to pay for that survey! And most of that land's so poor it wouldn't raise a fight!"

The assembly mumbled among themselves.

Crockett's ideas to take away lands claimed by speculators and resell them to the farmers at low prices — on extended terms — were outrageous. The representatives, many who had already invested sizable sums, intended to shape the bill to their particular preference. Crockett also proposed monies raised by the sales be used for development of a larger school system. Preposterous!

"Furthermore," David raised his voice above the muttering. "What little they have is to be wrested from them for the purpose of speculation, and a swindling machine is to be set up to strip them of what little the surveyors and warrant holders have left them. It shall never be said that I sat by in silence."

Eastern Whigs supported David's position, but Adams' administration used its' powerful influence to postpone the issue, never allowing it to come to a vote. Congressman Crockett did, however, manage a concession.

Fixing of land titles in his district was delayed for ten years, permitting farmers to purchase their own land as a right of preemption.

Even as David's bill lay straddled, he gained respect in the House.

He would also procure a new enemy. The irascible Andrew Jackson.

On March 7, 1829, Andrew Jackson was sworn in as the 7th President of the United States. His election in November outstripped Adams by 139,222 popular and 95 electoral votes.

Jackson entered the White House a grieving man. His wife Rachel had died of a heart attack in December, and he stilled dressed in deep mourning; black suit, white shirt and black tie, with a black band on his arm and another around his tall beaver hat.

For eight years, though he commanded the government with a zealous passion, this attire would rarely change.

In August of 1829, David Crockett was again elected to Congress.

Piqued by the re-election, Jackson worked to stay or defeat the Congressman's measures. The folly that proved a thorn in Adam's administration, now posed a threat to his own control of the country.

In 1830, the most important issue of that era came up for

vote. The Indian Removal Bill, a 19th century equivalent to the decadent Adolph Hitler's Final Solution.

Gold had been discovered in sections of Mississippi, Alabama, Georgia and Florida. This, coinciding with the best soil for growing cotton, brought in hundreds of land-hungry settlers. Indian villages were illegally entered and their residents dispossessed by force. Eager to continue a peaceful coexistence, the Indians offered little resistance. Tribes on these lands — Creeks, Cherokees, Chickasaws, Choctaws, Seminoles — moved out as white men moved in.

But authorities wanted all the tribes removed entirely from their states.

Faced with political pressure, President Jackson urged a bill to move the five tribes to unsettled lands west of the Mississippi. He also saw it as a way to line government coffers, while his cronies viewed it as a way to line their own. The rich lands would accrue to the United States, with covetous speculators garnering vast fortunes.

Congressman Crockett took a lonely opposition to the bill among members from Tennessee, his outspoken protests angering nearly everyone. Jackson, himself a Tennessean, cursed "that damned backwoodsman."

When asked why he chose to fight the government [1], David answered: "I don't wish t' represent m' feller citizens unless I cin act 'cordin' t' m' conscience."

Standing before the House, he spoke decisively [2]:

"I know I stand alone from my state. None of my colleagues agree with my sentiments, but if I should be the only member of the House who voted against the bill and the only man in the United States who disapproved of it, I would still vote against it, and it would be a matter of rejoicing till the day I died that I did.

"A treaty is the highest law of the land, but there are those who do not find it so. They want to juggle with the rights of the Indians and fritter them away. It's all wrong! It's not justice! I would rather be an old coon dog belonging to a poor man in the forest than belong to any party that will not do justice to all. These are the remnants of a once powerful people, and they must be fairly treated…"

David's arguments went unheard. The bill passed to President Jackson on May 28, 1830.

Between 1831 and 1838[3], the southeastern Indians were uprooted in what is sadly known as the Trail of Tears. Along the route hardships, disease and exposure took their toll. Approximately 3,500 died in the first year alone.

The winter of 1837-38 began the last removals. Some 15,000 to 17,000 Cherokees living in Georgia were pressed through Tennessee and Kentucky, across the frozen Ohio and Missouri Rivers, into the territory now known as Oklahoma. Nearly 4,000 died en route.

The Seminoles of Florida put up a resistance until all but a fleeing few were whipped from their ancestral home.

Thus closed one of the darkest pages in American history.

In 1831, Alexis de Tocqueville, a young French magistrate visiting America to study our penal system, witnessed the flight of a Choctaw tribe:

"…The old, the sick, the wounded, and newborns among

them, [were] forced to cross an ice-choked Mississippi River during the harsh winter. In the whole scene, there was an air of destruction, something which betrayed a final and irrevocable adieu; one couldn't watch without feeling one's heart wrung. The Indians have no longer a country, and soon will not be a people."

Traditional history observes the Cherokee migration to the Indian Territory as a singular Trail of Tears, yet all Native Americans to this day may justifiably dispute this viewing.

Unfortunately for whatever the basis, lost causes are seldom a means to personal advancement.

David's dissent of the removal bill fueled his defeat for re-election in 1831. Lawyer William Fitzgerald, strongly supported by the Jackson bloc, won in such a dirty campaign the ex-Congressman later remarked, "I should have punch'd 'li'l Fitz' in th' nose."

Back in his newly built home in Gibson County, Tennessee, David made plans for another stint in Congress. Defeat was not something he could tolerate, nor would he accept.

For the next two years he traveled throughout the district discussing troubling issues. He spoke with the young, the old, the women, zeroing on their interests and ideas.

Women had no vote, yet held influence over their men. By 1833, the voters — and their wives — were once more on his side.

He regained his seat in Congress.

David's popularity had increased in Washington during his hiatus. President Jackson, not a stupid man, knew it best to have the Congressman's alliance and invited him to the White House.

As David approached the wide archway a lackey, holding out his white-gloved hands to receive the Congressman's cap and coat, cried out with luster:

"Make way for Colonel Crockett!"

Removing and handing over his fur-lined cap but retaining his coat, his face devoid of a grin, David replied:

"Con'l Crockett cin make way f'r himself!"

What transpired between Jackson and Crockett that day had never been recorded. However, David was rumored to have told the President:

"Look't m' neck! Ya will not find there any collar with th' engravin', 'This dog belongs t' Andy Jackson'!"

Congressman Crockett was now a confirmed anti-Jackson man, opposing everything his administration stood for or against.

Jackson felt the twinge of a thorn vexing a rib.

In 1834, David read ***Sketches and Eccentricities of Col. David Crockett of West Tennessee.***

Anonymously written [4], this small publication embodied inaccuracies and ridicule of the man from the canebrake.

Nevertheless, its publisher was obliged to produce a second edition, newspapers printed excerpts, and booksellers of the day hustled to keep volumes in stock.

Resenting its appearance, he collaborated with Thomas Chilton to author ***A Narrative of David Crockett of the State of Tennessee, Written by Himself***.

In the spring of 1834, supported by the Whigs who whispered he might be a candidate for president against Martin Van Buren, David toured the major eastern cities.

Van Buren was Jackson's vice-president, and hand-picked to succeed him. In his naiveté, David relished thoughts of beating the "li'l red fox" if only to give "King Andrew I a boot in th' pants." Unaware he was merely a pawn in a bitter political game of chess.

The Whigs, endeavoring to unseat Jackson and his omnipotent clique, saw in David their opportunity. With his fervor for fame, vanity and virtue, and a deepening alienation from the present administration, who better to seduce than lovable Congressman Crockett — virtually a Robin Hood in buckskins. If he refused to wear Jackson's collar why couldn't they, who helped write his speeches and a best selling book, leash him as their own best-trained canine in Washington.

So they wined, dined, courted and flattered him. Loaned him money, laughed at his jokes, and sponsored his public appearances…

From Baltimore to Boston, crowds held out copies of his

autobiography for a signature. Everywhere, he was hailed as a young Benjamin Franklin.

In Philadelphia he was ceremoniously presented with a handsomely crafted chased rifle, made to his specifications, which he called "Beautiful Betsy" [5].

In Lowell, Massachusetts, he visited their famous mills, where: "[I] saw them make calico in beautiful colors; scarlet, blue and purple. Why, it was wonderful, the way they could turn out the calico so fast. It almost came up to the story of the old fellow who walked into a patent machine with a bundle of wool under one arm and came out t'other end with a new coat on."

From Boston he retraced his route through Pennsylvania, Ohio and Kentucky, with celebrations accompanying each step. "Go where I will," he told a member of his party, "ever'body seems anxious t' git a peep at me."

During this triumphal tour, he made speeches labeling Jackson "… a greater tyrant than Cromwell, Caesar, and Bonaparte." Though we must reason these the handiwork of his Whig sponsors, for it is doubtful he even knew who these infamous despots were.

David's second book, ***An Account of Col. Crockett's Tour to the North and Down East***, ghosted by Whig William Clark of Pennsylvania shortly following the tour, struck the bestseller list by the end of 1834.

Our 1800s comprised a period of myths and mythmakers. From Jim Bowie, to Kit Carson, to "Wild Bill" James Butler Hickcok, to Wyatt Earp incredible stories were journalistically manufactured, embellished and believed. And, of course, there was David "Davy" Crockett. With one exception. "Davy" created his own myths.

His tall tales and comical yarns made him an irrepressable legend in his own time and beyond.

Outstretched from his own imaginations came fabrications even wider, circulating not only throughout Tennessee and peoples of the East, but as far west as the Mexican province of Texas. If "Davy" said he could "grin a 'coon out'n a tree," it stretched to "No varmint cin 'scape Davy's grin." If he boasted to "totin' a steamship from th' banks o' th' Mississippi, with a rope slung o'er m' shoulder," it ripened into three, then four steamers trailing upriver.

An offshoot of this last tale had Davy traveling the Ohio River on a steamship.

When the motors ceased, the current drifting the vessel aimlessly toward certain damage, he got out and towed it upstream and over the falls.

Another fable branched from his ability to "ride a streak o' lightnin'."

When a comet raced threateningly across the sky, Davy climbed to the highest peak in the Allegheny Mountains and wrung off its fiery tail as it passed. Thereupon, saving the world from destruction.

"These were nothin' t' a man like Davy Crockett," added an old storyteller, casually lighting his pipe and gazing with sightless eyes into a dimming past.

Real life, unfortunately, is not such an easy yarn to spin.

A mysterious comet flamed untouched through the heavens in 1835. Long ago seen and feared by ancient Egyptians pursuing Moses to the Sea of Reeds, and later exalted by William the Conqueror in 1066 C.E., it would emerge to signify both defeat and victory.

For Congressman Crockett, it signaled defeat.

During David's eastern tour, Jacksonians had prepared an aggressive onslaught against his bid for a congressional fourth term.

The President himself chose his foe's opponent.

Adam "Timbertoes" Huntsman would be perfect for the job, peg-leg and all. Rough and rowdy and "as full of bull as Crockett," Huntsman availed his best chance to dash his enemy. Besides, if honest votes were not enough, $25 a head should put his man over the top.

Andrew Jackson could hate as hard as he could love.

In August, a narrow margin of 252 votes(4,652 to 4,400) brought David Crockett's political career to an end.

His Whig supporters swiftly turned their backs.

"I have announced through th' newspapers," he said at a dinner following the election. "That I never expect t' offer m' name again t' th' public fir any office. I hope t' spend th' ev'nin' in a social manner, leavin' politics out o' th' question..."

He finished with an embittered remark:

"Since ya have chosen t' elect a man with a timber toe t' succeed me, ya cin all go t' hell, an' I will go t' Texas!"

"It was expected of me to bow to the name of Andrew Jackson…even at the expense of my conscience and judgment. Such a thing was new to me, and a total stranger to my principles.

"I have acted fearlessly and independently, and I never will regret my course. I would rather be politically buried than be hypocritically immortalized."

David Crockett

Following his defeat for congressional re-election in 1835.

Part Three

The Alamo, Death...and Victory

Chapter 7

Contrary to oft-repeated versions, David Crockett did not leave for Texas as a freedom fighter. He simply intended on a new start. With John Wesley [1] practicing law in the Tennessee town of Paris, with Willie and "li'l Polly" grown and the others nearly, he felt safe entrusting his self-reliant wife to tend the younger children until his return.

He did not "…abandon his family to fight for glory," as contended by a small school of denigrating writers.

In fact, on October 31, 1835, he wrote to his brother-in-law, George Patton:

> **Dear Brother**
>
> **I have concluded to drop you a line. The whole connection is well. I am on the eve of starting to the Texes** [sic] **— on tomorrow morning. Myself, Abner Burgen, Lindsey K. Tinkle, & our nephew William Patton from the lower country — this will**

make our company. We will go through Arkinsaw [sic] **& I want to explore the Texes well before I return.**

David Crockett

Nowhere in this letter is there mention to joining a rebellion. To David, Texas was altogether a means to a prosperous new settlement. Nothing more.

And the price was right.

Even in the best of times, land in the United States cost $1.25 an acre at public auction, with cash payment needed for purchase. But in Texas 12 ½ cents an acre bought "the richest country in the world."

David pictured himself coming into his long-eluded fortune, then going home to "fetch th' family."

By the time David and his small group reached Arkansas, high-pitched voices heralded the news: "Con'l Crockett is a-comin'!" Villagers herded to greet and cheer the legendary Congressman from the East.

"Sorta makes me feel like a king, he winked at Lin Tinkle, dismounting in front of Little Rock's Jeffries Hotel.

A sizable crowd had gathered to escort the party in.

When David squeezed through the narrow doorway and claps on the back, his copper-colored skin turned white.

Before him extended a table arrayed with roasts of every kind. Though lacking a tablecloth, fine china and crystal stretched along its length. Noticing no knives, forks, or spoons, he chuckled: "Kinda reminds me o' th' time I went t' a banquet in Washington. I know'd what th' knives an' forks an' spoons were fir, but there wuz this funny li'l bowl with water in it. I poured a li'l whiskey in it an' drank it. An' wouldja know? They tol' me I jist drunk from m' finger bowl [2]."

Howling with laughter, everyone sat down to eat.

That evening, David danced with the ladies, was toasted by his hosts, and answered questions:

"Did you really wear buckskins when you was in Washington, Davy?"

"He prefers t' be called David," interrupted Lin Tinkle.

"Nope," David eyed Tinkle, whose grin lit up his reason for liking the man. "That's jist somethin' made up in those newspapers ya read. I look'd like jist 'bout ev'ry other Congressman."

"Why'd you lose the election?

" 'cause I couldn't tol'rate th' gov'nment no more. An' he know'd it."

"Did you really tell them all to go to hell?"

"Yep. An' that I wuz goin' t' Texas, too."

Reference to Texas stirred the big question.

"Are you going to fight for the Texas freedom from Mexico?"

"Wal, up t' now I haven't paid it much thought. But I've been hearin' a lot o' talk lately. I may have some idle time on my hands 'fore I settle down. So if th' Texians need a helpin' hand on their high road t' freedom, I reck'n I'll lend it t' 'em. I've always lik'd t' git my spoon in a mess o' that kind. Fir if there's anythin' in th' world worth livin' fir, it's freedom."

The following day, David and his three companions set out for the Red River country on the Texas border.

On January 5th, he and William Patton crossed the Sabine River into Nacogdoches, Texas. Four days later, David returned to the little post of San Augustine, at the Red River, where Lin Tinkle and Abner Burgen had decided to return home on January 4th.

Dated January 9th, he wrote his first — and last — letter from Texas:

Saint Augusteen [sic]
Jan. 9, 1836

Dear Son & Daughter

This is the first time I have had the opportunity to write you with convenience. I am now blessed with excellent health & am in high spirits. Although I have had many difficulties to encounter I have gone through safe & have been received by everybody with open arms of friendship. I am hailed with a hearty welcome to this country, a dinner & a party of ladys [sic] **have honored me with an invitation to partisipate** [sic] **with them both at Nacindocher** [Nacogdoches] **& this place; the cannon was fired here on my arrival &I must say as to what I seen of Tex-**

es [sic] it is the garden spot of the world; the best land & the best prospects for health I have ever saw is here & I do believe it is a fortune to any man to come here; there is a world of country to settle, it is not required to pay down for your league of land; every man is entitled to his headright of 4,438 acres; they may make the money to pay off the land.

I have great hope of getting the agency to settle that country & I would be glad to see every friend I have settle there, it would be a fortune to them all.

I have taken the oath of the Government & have enrolled my name as a volunteer for six months & will set out for the Rio Grande in a few days with the volunteers of the U.S., but all volunteers is entitled to a vote for a member of the Convention & these members are to be voted for; & I have but little doubt of being elected a member to form the Convention for this province.

I am rejoiced by my fate, I had rather be in my present situation than be elected to Congress for life. I am in hopes of making a fortune for myself & family, bad has been my prospects.

I have not wrote [sic] to William, but have requested John to direct him what to do. I hope you show him this letter & also

your Brother John, as it is not convenient at this time to write to them.

I hope that you will all do the best you can & I will do the same. Do not be uneasy about me, I am with my friends. I must close with great respect, your affectionate father, Farewell.

David Crockett [3]

This letter indicates substantially David's plans to fare in this land. By swearing allegiance to the sovereign nation of Texas, he opened a way for election to its Continental Convention. As a volunteer in the Texas army, he received a promise of 640 acres in free land.

It was a gamble. A gamble that would have paid off had not Antonio López de Santa Anna been preparing to cross the Rio Grande.

An interesting description of David Crockett during his passage to Texas was given by Isabelle Gordon, an 87-year-old widow who had met the Tennessee party when a young woman in the town of Clarksville, Arkansas [4].

"Crockett was dressed like a perfect gentleman, and not as a backwoodsman. He did wear a coonskin cap [5]. It has always disgusted me to read these accounts of Crockett that characterize him as an ignorant backwoodsman. Neither in dress, conversation, nor bearing could he have created the impression that he was ignorant or uncouth. He was a man of wide, practical information, and was dignified and entertaining. He was a gentleman all over."

This account offers further evidence that David Crockett left for Texas in search of affluence. Not as a revolutionary.

Though he left Tennessee clad for hunting, throughout most of Arkansas and into Nacogdoches his buckskins were neatly packed in one saddlebag, along with his fiddle. The other contained a jug of corn whiskey. And, even though he carried two extra rifles to anticipate any trouble along his route, Ol' Betsy was safely sheathed throughout most of the trip.

Returning to Nacogdoches, David joined with Captain William Harrison, recruited about twelve excited volunteers, called them his "Tennessee boys," and headed for the town of San Antonio de Béxar by way of Washington-on-the-Brazos.

San Antonio de Béxar — known today simply as San Antonio — is located 150 miles north of the Rio Grande.

In 1718, Don Martín de Alarcon established the Villa de Béxar near the newly built mission of San Antonio de Valero.

This mission, together with four similar structures strung along the San Antonio River bank, comprised Spain's attempt to press Christianity on local Indians. Between 1744 and 1756, a convent, whitewashed outer walls and a large chapel were erected. However, by 1793, either from disease or from the Indian's reluctance to accept Spanish dominion, San Antonio de Valero was abandoned to the elements.

In 1801, Spanish-Mexican troops arrived from Pueblo de San Carlos del Alamo de Parris, in northern Mexico, to occupy the mission against Apache and Comanche raiders preying on surrounding settlements. Though her protective outer walls had fallen into disrepair, and the mission herself lay threadbare, the soldiers worked tirelessly to fortify.

Her living quarters, once housing Franciscan friars and their Indian converts, were transformed into a barracks, the chapel into an armory. When she was finished they proudly renamed her for their post in Mexico, affectionately called the Alamo [6].

The Alamo was now a military fort, situated just east of the San Antonio River, overlooking Béxar.

Secured by her presence, its citizens breathed a sigh of relief for twenty-four years.

Then, in 1825, she stood once again mysteriously empty.

And would remain so until December 5, 1835, when General Martín Perfecto de Cos, Santa Anna's inept brother-in-law, with a force of 1,100 Mexican regulars against a little over 300 Texian volunteers, retreated behind her walls to raise the white flag of surrender on December 9th.

With Cos returned home in disgrace, the Texians moved into the sprawling fortress.

By the end of December, Texas was entirely cleared of Mexican soldiers.

Convinced that war was over, that separation from Mexico imminent, most of the volunteers returned to their farms and ranches. Even their commander, Major General Edward Burleson, rode smugly out of the Alamo, as a lonely wind wailed her discontent.

Three hundred and four remained under the command of a young Colonel Frank Johnson.

Drawn by melancholy chords they felt compelled to stay, as if the old mission-turned-fort cried out for fellowship.

Early in January, Colonel James Clinton Neill replaced an edgy Johnson.

As Johnson left with orders from Colonel James Walker Fannin, Jr. to invade the Mexican port city of Matamoros, depleting the sad friary of a reluctant 200, Neill set to proceed with orders from General Sam Houston.

Houston wanted all artillery removed and the fort blown up. But the one hundred and four men continuing under Neill begged him not to do it. Strangely, he complied.

On January 19th, Colonel James Bowie arrived with a contingent of 30 men. In his hand, he held even stronger orders:

"Completely demolish the mission, salvage the guns, then retreat to Goliard."

Although he knew, as did Neil, the Alamo could hardly withstand an enemy assault; there was something about her brooding walls that made him tear up the orders.

When Colonel William Barret Travis entered on February 3rd, with another 30 men, he carried the same orders from provincial governor, Henry Smith.

However, Bowie had already written to Governor Smith on February 2nd:

> **The salvation of Texas depends in great measure on keeping Béxar out of the hands of the enemy. It stands on the frontier piquet guard; and if it was in the possession of Santa Anna, there is no strong-hold from which to repel him in his march on the Sabine** [River]. **Colonel Neill and myself have come to the solemn resolution that we will rather die in these ditches than give them up to the enemy.**

Travis and Bowie disliked each other since they both entered Texas, but in this they concurred. The mission San Antonio de Valero, if a crumbling ruin, needed to be spared.

The north winds quieted into silence. The old Alamo felt secure at last. She was among friends.

Meanwhile, General Santa Anna, enraged by his brother-in-law's defeat in December, marched his troops unmercifully toward the Rio Grande.

On February 8th, news of David Crockett's appearance in Béxar reached Travis, Bowie and Neill.

"Time for a celebration," said Bowie.

"You'd celebrate anything," chided Travis, having heard

of Bowie's unsavory reputation.

Neill watched in muted fascination when Bowie thundered that Travis was a "Damned perfumed sissy."

William Barret 'Buck" Travis, a young, tall, good-looking — if somewhat shallow — lawyer, had fled ingloriously from Alabama following the death of his wife's lover.

Whether he killed the man or not is for newer study. We only know that when he passed into Texas in 1831, he left a pregnant wife and 2-year-old son back home in Claiborne.

Born on August 9, 1809 in Edgefield County (now Saluda County), South Carolina, Travis grew up in Alabama.

By the time he was twenty, he was practicing law, teaching, and wed to a Rosanna Cato. When rumor spread that his wife had a lover, the man was found dead. Not wishing to face prosecution for murder, he abandoned everything and took up residence in Texas.

With his past securely locked, as he believed, he signed the Mexican oath as "single" and later as a "widow."

An unadulterated romantic, Travis believed his destiny lay in "a splendid future, or an early death."

When hostilities with Mexico mounted, he boldly placed his name with the "War Party" and spoke for independence.

Commissioned a regular army lieutenant colonel, courtesy of General Stephen Austin, he rode off to battle…

Bowie considered Travis more a lover than a fighter. But what sort of a lover, he wondered. With his habit of coiling his auburn locks scented with lavender perfumes, there was something strange about the man…

Half-horse, half-alligator — and bit of a tarnished hero — James "Jim" Bowie was Kentucky-born on April 10, 1796, and raised in the Louisiana bayou.

By eighteen, he was roping and riding alligators.

Over the next two decades, with his brothers John and Rezin, Jr., Jim made a fortune in slave trade and land speculations. In two years alone, the brothers divided $65,000 smuggling slaves for the well-known buccaneer, Jean Lafitte.

As speculators, the brothers traded in shady certificates, selling allegedly secured lands in the Arkansas Territory. However, when the Supreme Court discovered their little scheme, pronouncing the land titles "forged and fraudulent," the boys were out of business.

Jim Bowie stood 6′ 1″, weighed 180 pounds in his prime, had thick reddish-brown hair with sideburns, and steel-gray eyes. Though not as powerful as David Crockett he was, nevertheless, agile and tough. Some called him a killer, while others labeled him a product of his time. Whatever the case, he was a feared duelist throughout the South and Southwest. In one such duel he killed the son of Jean Lafitte; in another crippled the hand of notorious gambler, "Bloody" Sturdivant. "I've never started a fight," he once boasted, "but I'll be damned if I'll ever be beaten in one."

Still, the foundation for his fame as a fighter rests on just two encounters. The first erupted near Natchez, on a Mississippi River sandbar, in 1827.

A pair of pistol duelists, Samuel Levi Wells III and Dr. Thomas Harris Maddox, squared off to settle a grudge. Both fired, and missed. Thereupon, disgruntled fighting broke out among the opposing ten seconds, of which Bowie was one.

Armed with an ineffective pistol and a butcher knife [7], he was shot in the hip and shoulder, stabbed in the chest, then clubbed about the head and shoulders.

Before collapsing he gutted a Sheriff Norris Wright of Rapedes Parish, slashed another to ribbons, and helped rout the remaining opposing seconds.

The second took place in Texas in 1830. By then he was expertly skilled in his use of the Bowie knife.

Three knife-wielding assassins [8], hired by Sturdivant to avenge his crippling, ambushed him on the streets of Béxar. The first assailant to reach him was nearly beheaded when Bowie sliced horizontally with the heavy blade. The next inflicted a leg wound before his belly was torn open. The third attempted to flee, but Bowie, as one eyewitness to the fracas put it, "split his skull to the shoulders with a single blow [of his knife]."

Restlessly pursuing land and money, Bowie had first drifted into Texas in 1828. Characteristically bypassing the poor Anglo-American settlements, he later chose the rich Mexican citizenship of San Antonio de Béxar for a permanent residence.

He also chose a wife.

Maria Ursula de Veramendi was the beautiful 19-year-old daughter of Don Juan Martín de Veramendi, recently elected vice-governor of the Coahuila y Tejas province.

Pretending as an American gentleman of opulence, Jim ingratiated himself into the Veramendi family.

So charmed were they with his wit and grace, they sponsored him into the Catholic Church — a requirement for Mexican citizenship — and the Don offered him a partnership in his many business ventures.

The courtship of James "Jim" Bowie and Ursula de Veramendi soon followed.

On April 25, 1831, they exchanged vows at San Fernando Church, Béxar.

Within weeks of the marriage, using his phony holdings in Arkansas as collateral, Jim borrowed enough of his father-in-law's money to buy nearly 50,000 acres of land at 5¢ an acre. He then persuaded Veramendi's Mexican friends to invest in eleven leagues each (48,712 acres), and sell the titles back to him at a profit.

At the age of 35, Jim Bowie held 750,000 acres of Texas land almost legally [9].

In the beginning, Bowie's marriage tended toward the fiscal, rather than the romantic.

Veramendi liked his new son-in-law, but would not cast caution to the wind. Bowie was a foreigner and nationally notorious. In order for the groom to receive continued support, he would have to sign a marriage contract. In it, Bowie — not Ursula — would furnish a dowry of $15,000.

Bowie signed it with flourishing swirls, misrepresenting his age as 30 instead of 35, while listing his assets at nearly a quarter of a million dollars.

He failed to mention, however, that $98,000 of the assets were notes from purchasers of his fraudulent Arkansas land titles.

Jim settled down long enough to give Ursula two children, Marie Elve, born March 20, 1832, and James Veramendi, born July 18, 1833, then was off in search of the fabled San Saba silver mines.

Since 1828, he had been seeking them; not realizing the mines existed solely in wishful imaginations.

In 1826, cholera broke out in Lower Bengal, gradually moving along trade routes to the American Continent. By 1832, the epidemic was in St. Louis. A Mississippi steamer steered it down to New Orleans. Another ship brought it westward. Jim was in Natchez, himself sick in bed, when he heard the news. Ursula and the children, along with her father and mother, were dead within three days of contracting the disease.

Ursula's uncle, José Antonio Navarro, wrote to a mutual friend, Lieutenant Samuel M. Williams, holding that he had "no heart to break the news to Señor Bowie":

> **When I told you my fears of the cholera it looks as if I had a premonition, because my brother-in-law, Verimendi** [sic]**, my sister Josefa, his wife, and Ursula Bowie and her children, died unexpectedly in Monclova**

...

> **Three days illness were enough, from the 5th to the 8th of this month** [September], **to end all these precious lives...**

Bowie returned to the cool mountain air of Monclova, Mexico, where Veramendi kept a summer home. He had urged Ursula to take the children and her parents to this safe, healthful retreat... "But Jamie, why you cannot come with us? Must you go away, again?" "I have important business. There's nothing to worry about" ... Now he wept above their graves. The only prayer he knew was the Lord's. He was unable to say it. Guilt choked his voice.

From then on, it was a slide for Jim Bowie. His drunkenness became as well known as his legendary fighting prowess. For a time he went to his mother's home in Louisiana for solace. Then he decided to head back to Texas. He was lost in heart and soul. Before leaving Louisiana, he made out his will. With the gentle touch of his wife's hand on his cheek forever gone from his life...

... Yet when he reached Texas, he appeared a changed man. Though still drinking heavily, his thoughts had a purpose. Having no further ties with Mexico, he scorned the "meanness and duplicity" suffered by Anglo-Americans trying to forge a life "on this new frontier."

In a speech before the Texas Consultation in 1835, he said:

"Yielding to the dictates of my heart, I had taken to my bosom a true and lovely woman of a different country, the daughter of a distinguished Coahuila-Texian. Yet, as a thief in the night, death had invaded my home and taken away my wife, my little ones, and my father-in-law. Now, standing alone of all of my blood in Texas, all I ask is the privilege of serving it in the field."

Following these words, life held new import for James "Jim" Bowie. He would celebrate everything with a drink, scheme for ever-larger holdings in Texas land, and "…be damned if I'll let that tyrant Santa Anna take it away from me!"

Commissioned a colonel in the People's Army of Texas, he believed he had the power to grapple the entire Mexican country…

"Well, boys," said Neill, walking to the door as his two younger officers tried to glare each other down. "Let's go see what Colonel Crockett has to say about our situation."

David Crockett, fully attired in buckskins, was mounted on a packing crate regaling the gathered Béxarians with a repertoire of jokes, boasts and exaggerations when the three colonels entered the Main Plaza. For the first time in days, Travis laughed. He liked Crockett immediately. Bowie eyed the big Tennessean he had heard so much about. He, too, decided there was nothing to dislike about the man. Laughing and clapping vigorously until a coughing spasm bent him over, he found it hard to believe that anyone would drink from a finger bowl.

Then, surprisingly, David concluded on a serious note:

"… I have come to aid you all I can in your noble cause.

"I shall identify myself with your interests, and all the honor that I desire is that of defending as a high private, in common with my fellow citizens, the liberties of our common country [10]."

Everyone, including the inveterately self-absorbed William "Buck" Travis, stared in awe. The jester had transmuted to an eloquent orator.

David jumped from the crate. Travis and Bowie introduced themselves and grabbed his hand. Bowie slapped him on the back, and all three sashayed to the cantina, followed by cheering and yelling citizens and volunteers alike.

Colonel Neill returned to the Alamo.

Like many able second-raters, when at least two legendary figures come together, he was nudged aside.

On February 10th, a fandango jammed Béxar to welcome the new arrivals. David brought out his fiddle and scratched a Virginia reel. Dogs in the street swung their muzzles heavenward and howled for mercy. No one noticed. They were too drunk.

The festivities were still in full sway when a courier rode in around 1 a.m. with news of the latest Mexican advance. Santa Anna neared the Rio Grande.

Bowie, Travis and Crockett, ignoring Neill, huddled over the message. But, deeming it's warning trivial, resumed the celebration.

Corn whiskey and beer continued to flow. Travis danced with one señorita after another. David dueled his ever trusty fiddle with Scotsman John McGregor's bagpipes. Even the attending Mexicans, who never quite understood the Anglo-American ways, cheered with delight.

"You know, Crockett," said Bowie when David sat beside him to rest. He was 49. Not as young as he used to be. "I guess I had it wrong about Travis. I haven't seen him dance with a muchacho all night."

David looked at Bowie with raised, confused, eyebrows.

Bowie slapped his knee and guffawed until seized by a rasping cough. Reaching for a handkerchief to wipe his mouth, he peeked at its contents, then stuffed it quickly back into his pocket. It wouldn't do for Crockett to see he had just spit up blood.

On the 11th, Neill left for a "twenty day leave." His excuses ranged from sickness in the family, to a need to raise defense funds. But, in reality, he knew it was time to relinquish his post.

Rankled by last night's snub, he threw saddle and gear on his horse and mounted.

"I leave you in temporary command," he had told Travis.

Though this seemed to imply Neil's plan to return, Travis sensed he would not. Leaning on a rail, he visually surveyed the old mission they had been strengthening for days, and smiled. A lot of effort was still needed. Yet with Green Jameson, his chief engineer, leading work crews both day and night the Alamo was shaping into a fort.

Travis' satisfied musings were interrupted by a hoarse voice behind him.

"He had no right to turn this garrison over to you," Bowie flushed angrily.

Actually, the Alamo began her fortification as far back as January 22nd. Long before Travis appeared on the scene.

Neill, Bowie and Green Jameson, a Kentucky-born lawyer from San Felipe turned post engineer, employed insurmountable energies in readying her for defense.

Jameson, especially, proved most imaginative. He built a palisade of heavy logs to close a 75-foot gap in the southeast angle — considered the weakest point — between the chapel and Low Barracks, constructed a semi-circular "lunette"[11] to guard the main gate on the south, threw up platforms of dirt and wood along the wall to serve as parapets and gun mounts, and put an 18-pound cannon in the southwest corner to overlook approach from Béxar. He also placed guns, extending from 4 to 12-pounders, at different strategic points about the compound. A pair of 8-pounders was stationed in the plaza near the south gate, as last-ditch weapons should the Mexicans break through.

A spark ignited lethargic, waned spirits. Ragged, ill-fed, disillusioned souls had come from limbo, as if the mission San Antonio de Valero called for assistance.

The place soon hummed with excitement. Dormant abilities were reanimated.

Captain Almeron Dickinson, a Gonzales hat maker and part-time blacksmith, re-found his knack for handling artillery. He took charge of the guns left by Cos in December.

John Baugh of Virginia, with his officious nature accepted the position as adjutant.

Hiram Williamson of Philadelphia, having a love for bellowing orders, was chosen drillmaster.

On February 9th, Jameson inspected the fort. Work still needed completion, specifically in the chapel where most of its roof had collapsed in the 1760s. Why wasn't it fixed when that Spanish Flying Company occupied it against Indian attacks? Who's to understand their minds, anyway? No matter. Given time, he'd do it.

Checking the southeast breastwork, he thought back to the time he had first appraised the Alamo.

That day he wrote to Sam Houston:

You can plainly see that the Alamo never was built by a military people for a fortress.

What Jameson saw that day was a large compound ranging over three acres. In its center was a rectangular ground, bordered by walls and huts, charitably called "the plaza." This plaza was approximately the size of a city block.

A one-story building called the "Low Barracks" stood on the south side, pierced by the main entrance. The west side, facing Béxar about 400 yards, contained a string of adobe huts protected by a 12-foot high stonewall. Along the north side ran a similar wall.

The strongest edifice seemed to be the two-story "Long Barrack," housing a second floor hospital, which banked the east side. However, though protected by the wall cornered from the north and bordered by a large corral to the rear, it fell far short of reaching the south side of the plaza. Within this gap, between the Long Barrack and the southeast angle of the compound, lay the Alamo chapel [12].

From years of neglect, the chapel was now in ruins. Still, close examination proved it the yard's sturdiest building. Although its central roof had long since vanished, the sacristy and small rooms along one side were still intact. The walls were four to five feet thick, which would repel heavy bombardment. The front doors were of heavy oak. Debris clustered in the center — due to Cos' ineffectual attempt at fortification in December — could also be used to advantage.

Unfortunately, the chapel was set too far back from the south wall. A glaring gap of seventy-five feet in the southeast corner would render its durability trivial. The break would have to be checked with timber high and strong enough to rebuff a direct assault.

Jameson smacked the solid wood. Still the weakest station," he reminded himself, "but if we have some good men posted here…"

"What do you think?" asked Bowie, walking up to stand beside him.

Travis came up to ask the same question.

"Colonels," answered Jameson with a merry twinkle in his eye. " A month ago I wouldn't have believed it. But if we position our artillery in the right direction, we can whip the Mexicans ten-to-one."

"I said, Neill had no right to put you in charge!" shouted Bowie.

"Might I remind you, sir, that Neill and I are regular army?"

Travis spoke slowly, deliberately, as one would address an obtuse child.

"And I'm only a volunteer, right?" Might I inform you, sir, that I outrank you by seniority? I'm 40! While you, sir, must be no more than 28!"

"Twenty-six."

"So shoot me for a liar. Crockett, come over here!"

David reluctantly ambled over and leaned against the rail next to Bowie and Travis. It creaked with his weight.

"I suppose you heard our conversation?" Bowie pulled out his handkerchief and wiped his mouth.

"So'd th' whole camp, Con'l."

"Well, so what do you think?"

"Wal, 'pears t' me," drawled Crockett, as if working up to a political speech, "that none o' th' reg'lar army wants t' listen t' you, Con'l Bowie. On t'other hand, neither will th' volunteers listen t' you, Con'l Travis. So why not compromise? That's a word I learnt in Washington. You, Con'l Bowie, take charge o' th' volunteers. An you, Con'l Travis, do th' same with th' reg'lar army."

Travis was furious.

"Preposterous! Everybody knows I should be in charge!"

"Wal, then. Let's take it t' a vote," grinned Crockett.

The votes were cast in favor of David Crockett's suggestion. Travis and Bowie would operate as co-commanders.

Travis marched off to sulk in true military fashion.

"I think we made the con'l mad," said David, taking off his cap and fingering through his long, graying-dark, hair.

"He'll be fine in a few days. He always does that when he doesn't get his way."

Bowie smiled toward the retreating Travis, then looked at David.

"How about you, Crockett? Who's orders will you follow?"

"Wal, Con'l," David picked up Ol' Betsy and made an about-face. "Since I'm jist here t' help out, I'll listen t' anybody."

Bowie's shrill laughter behind him turned into a grating cough.

Travis, however, was too angry to let this insult pass.

Unable to endure further humiliation, he wrote to Governor Smith on February 13th:

> **Bowie was elected co-commander by two small companies & since his election he has been roaring drunk all the time; has assumed all command — and is proceeding in a most disorderly & irregular manner & turning everything topsy-turvy.**
>
> **If I did not feel my honor & and that of my country compromised I would leave here instantly for some other point with the troops under my immediate command. I am unwilling to be responsible for the drunken irregularities of any man.**

Travis referred to Bowie's actions of the 12th and 13th when, his resistance lowered by the consumption absorbing his once powerful body, he burst into town on a drunken binge.

Loudly claiming command of the entire garrison, he accosted private citizens and ordered Béxar officials to empty the calaboose of all prisoners. When one was remanded to custody, he blew into a blind rage and, calling his men from the Alamo, paraded them back and forth along the Main Plaza. Soon, they were as drunk as he. Waving their rifles, shouting and hooting.

On the 14th, Bowie awoke with a tremendous hangover. Sheepishly, he went to the indignant Travis and tendered an agreement. They would keep their separate commands, but make all major decisions together.

"Crockett was right," Bowie offered Travis his hand, "Your men won't listen to me, and mine won't listen to you. Such a thing won't do. Unity is more important than personal ambition."

Jointly, they dispatched a letter to Governor Smith:

> **There is no doubt that the enemy will shortly advance upon this place, and that this will be the first point of attack. We must therefore urge the necessity of sending reenforcements as speedily as possible to our aid.**
>
> [signed] **William Barret Travis**
> [signed] **James Bowie**
> **Co-Comdts**

On the morning of February 22nd, Santa Anna buckled

on a $7,000 sword, mounted a gold-trimmed saddle, and waved his tired army toward the last leg of its grueling trek.

San Antonio de Béxar beckoned Mexico's "Napoléon of the West."

She would not have long to wait.

In the early hours of Tuesday, February 23rd, a muddied messenger steamed into Béxar with news that the Mexican army approached.

Béxar would be attacked today.

Citizens must evacuate immediately!

By sunrise oxcarts laden with clothing, bedding, pots and pans creaked in a slow but steady stream to the sanctuary of an open countryside. Those unable to afford the luxury of carts gladly walked, bending under their heavy burden.

Travis, in his little room in town, awoke to the sound of bumping, rattling and muffled voices beneath his window. Damn! The citizens are leaving. In droves! But why? According to his calculations, Santa Anna wasn't due until April; the middle of March at the earliest. Sure, he had been warned twice — on February 10th and February 20th — that the Mexicans were on the move. But even that despotic leader wouldn't risk losing most of his army, horses and supplies attempting to cross the Rio Grande in dead of winter. He would wait until spring. Damn!

Rushing into the street, he pulled a cart to a stop and asked where they were going.

"To the country, Colonel Travis."

"To do a little farming, Colonel Travis."

Farming? By townspeople? In February?

Frustrated by the obvious lies, he ordered no one else to leave.

Frenzied citizens objected. Some were arrested, some questioned at random. Others rumbled back to their homes, only to sneak out by a rarely used road. If the Anglo-Americans desired to die, that was one thing. They had no wish to.

Travis' questioning revealed nothing until 11 a.m. that morning when Nathaniel Lewis, a Béxar merchant, told of a courier who had warned them to get out of town. The Mexican cavalry, they learned, was only eight miles away.

Tearing to the San Fernando Church with Dr. John Sutherland, a physician newly arrived from Alabama, and Daniel Cloud, Travis took the steps to its belfry two at a time.

Though an unimpressive structure the church, slumbering peacefully between the Main and so-called Military Plaza, dominated the area. From its lofty, square tower, one could see for miles in every direction.

Straining anxious eyes toward the south and west, the three could see the chaparral, the mesquite thickets, and the empty plains. Nothing more.

Stationing Cloud to ring the bell if anything looked suspicious, Travis and Sutherland clattered back down to the street.

Cloud scanned the rolling prairies, rays from the resplendent morning sun causing him to squint. He had lost his hat somewhere in one of the cantinas last night so, removing his jacket he fashioned it over his head to form a visor and settled for the watch.

Daniel William Cloud had entered Béxar as one of David Crockett's "Tennessee boys."

The 22-year-old Kentucky lawyer met David in Nacogdoches on January 8th. As an idealist, he yearned to join a cause. Any cause. So when Crockett said on January 14th that he was "gonna fight Santy Anny," that there was always room for a good companion, he was drawn like a magnet.

Today, though, he wondered if his actions were not too impetuous.

But there was no time to think of that now. Light glinted off something in the distance. Lances! The Mexican Cavalry!

"Oh, my God! There must be a thousand of them!"

Grabbing the bell rope, he pulled as hard as he could, clamoring peels resounding throughout the town and into the hills. Men poured from houses, cantinas… Everywhere.

Scrambling to the tower, Sutherland close on his heels, Travis looked over the horizon.

"Where, man?"

"There! The enemy is in view, sir!" Shouted Cloud, excitedly pointing southwest.

Travis peered out. Nothing!

"False alarm!" He yelled down from the belfry.

The men below dispersed, cursing the stupid sentry.

"I seen them, sir!" insisted Cloud. They've hid behind the brushwood!"

"Sure! More likely you dreamed them. Stay awake! And take that silly thing off your head!"

"Ignoramus," muttered an angry Cloud as Travis descended the stairs. "Who is he, anyway? Jim Bowie's my commander. He would have believed me. Crockett would have believed me."

Sutherland regarded Cloud for a moment, then turned and followed Travis down the winding grade.

"I believe him, Colonel!" said Sutherland, stepping beside Travis as they both reached the street.

"Why not give me a good man who knows the area, and we'll check it out."

Travis turned to look back at the church. Cloud still had his jacket tied around his head.

"All right, Doctor," he sighed. "Take that redhead 'Smitty.' The one they call El Colorado. He's been here over five years. He should know the country."

As Sutherland and John W. Smith, a versatile entrepreneur from Missouri, mounted their horses, Travis pulled on Sutherland's reins.

"Remember, Doctor. If we see you coming back at anything but a slow gait, we'll know that Cloud was indeed right. Head for the Alamo."

Travis slapped Sutherland's horse on the rump and apprehensively watched his two riders trot westward along the

Laredo branch of the Camino Real.

Little over a mile out of town, Sutherland and Smith maneuvered south toward the Alazan hills, where Cloud said he had seen the cavalry.

Quietly alighting their horses and making their way up a slope to its summit, they gazed down at a sight that chilled their very bones.

Just over the crest, less than 150 yards, close to 400 lancers in polished armor twisted and turned their mounts in a restless line; apparently awaiting orders for a next stage of operation.

Cloud was right!

Scrambling down the hill to their horses, the frenzied men spurred for home at top speed.

Smith was in a distant lead, while Sutherland was having trouble. His smooth-shod bay mare could not handle the slick, muddy road left by last night's rainfall. In a scramble of slipping and sliding, he somersaulted to the ground, the animal landing across his legs. Smith raced back to help, as the dazed horse clambered to her feet. Grabbing his shaken comrade, Smith helped him to stand.

Though badly hurt, Sutherland managed to regain his saddle and four frantic bodies coursed pell-mell for town.

A vindicated Daniel Cloud spied the oncoming riders and clanged his bell without stopping.

Captain Almeron Dickinson rode at breakneck speed to his quarters in the home of Ramón Musquiz, where his 22-year-old wife Susanna waited with little Angelina clutched nervously in her arms.

"The Mexicans are upon us, Sue. Give me the baby and jump up behind me."

Potrero Street, which led to a footbridge spanning the San Antonio River, was already crowded. So, in guiding his horse south of the bridge, Dickinson urged it through shallow water, coming out near the south entrance to the Alamo.

Jim Bowie highballed it to the Veramendi house, where his late wife's cousin Juana and her adopted sister, Gertrudis, fretfully tread its burnished stone floor. Juana, married to an Anglo-American doctor named Alsbury, held tightly to her baby. Where was her husband when she needed him?

"To the Alamo!" shouted Bowie. "Let's go!"

David Crockett, conducting the exodus, met Sutherland and Smith as they galloped into the Main Plaza.

"Travis is already at th' Alamo," he pointed to the east. "th' whole garrison is headed 'cross th' bridge. As soon as ever'body's safely 'cross, I'll follow."

Trinidad Saucedo, 27-year-old servant in the Veramendi house, clung desperately to a garrison member as he sweated toward the fortress.

As the garrison and hangers-on streamed across the narrow bridge and on to the Alamo, the remaining Mexican townspeople shook their heads with a pang of sympathy:

"Poor devils, they'll all be killed."

Swarming into the Alamo, each man took his position.

The women and children were escorted to the smaller rooms in the chapel.

Although the safest shelter for the innocents, there was still some danger. The fort's entire gunpowder supply was stored across from these rooms.

Travis set up headquarters in an adobe hut in the west wall. Time was running out, he knew. And still no reinforcements. Why hadn't he listened to the two previous warnings? Why hadn't he listened to Bowie? Bowie told him Santa Anna wouldn't wait until April…

Too late now, he decided.

Dashing off a short appeal to Fannin at Goliard, he handed the message to a young courier named Johnson.

As Johnson pushed through the door to his mission, David clomped in with Dr. Sutherland leaning on his shoulder. Sutherland's knee, severely injured in the early afternoon fall, had stiffened and his leg was now completely useless.

Still, he could sit a horse. He could ride to Gonzales and rally the people there.

"Good," said Travis.

David helped Sutherland to a chair, then strutted over to Travis' scarred old desk.

"Wal, Con'l. Here I am. Assign me t' someplace, an' me an' m' Tennessee boys will defend it all right."

"I have just the place for you, Crockett. The southeast wall. It's the weakest point, but I'm sure the world's greatest hunter shouldn't have any trouble. You are the world's greatest hunter? Aren't you, Crockett?"

"I wish t' be shot, Con'l," grinned David, feeling himself as young as 'Davy,' "if'n I'm not."

Turning on his heels, he saluted Dr. Sutherland and left the room.

Travis chuckled as the buckskinned soldier departed.

"What a character," he muttered to himself. "If we had a garrison full of Crocketts, we wouldn't need guns. We could laugh the Mexicans to death."

Blithely shaking his head at this surprising attempt at humor, Travis grabbed his quill and burned a paper with five brisk sentences:

> **The enemy in large force is in sight. We want men and provisions. Send them to us. We have 150 men and are determined to defend the Alamo to the last. Give us assistance.**

He addressed the note to "Andrew Ponton, Judge, Gonzales."

Then scratched it out and wrote:

"To any of the inhabitants of Texas."

Handing this short script to Sutherland, he helped the doctor to his feet and out to his horse, where John W. Smith awaited his companion for a race to Gonzales. It was a little after 3 p.m., February 23rd.

At 3 p.m., February 23rd, Santa Anna majestically entered San Antonio de Béxar. It was 1813 all over again. Then, as a 19-year-old lieutenant under General Joaquín de Arredondo of the Spanish army, he had heroically crushed a rebel uprising in the Battle of Medina.

General Arredondo had given him orders he would never forget "…Since the foreigners [rebels] are making war, they are due no consideration and will be given no quarter."

He followed these instructions to the letter.

Now, twenty-three years later, he was ready to follow his own instructions.

Signaling his standard-bearers, they unfurled a blood-red flag and placed it high atop the tower — flapping and snapping in the afternoon breeze — of San Fernando Church.

Visible to the occupants of the Alamo, it signified one thing. No mercy!

From the Alamo, Travis ordered her 18-pound cannon fired; its ball bouncing harmlessly into town, hitting no one.

It was simply a loud exclamation mark of defiance!

Jim Bowie, alarmed by Travis' imprudent act, seized a paper and scribbled an apology to Santa Anna in Spanish. He was beginning to wonder the wisdom of defiance if any possibility for negotiation remained.

Green Jameson carried the plea into town to find out if in fact this were conceivable.

Santa Anna raged.

"Who do these rebels think they are? Offering to negotiate as equals?"

Tossing the paper to his military assistant, Colonel José Batres, he strode over to view the old mission, a malicious smile on his face.

Colonel Batres answered Bowie:

> **As the Aide-de-Camp of His Excellency, the President of the Republic, I reply to you according to the order of His Excellency, that the Mexican Army cannot come to terms under any condition with rebellious foreigners to whom there is no other recourse left, if they wish to save their lives, than to place themselves immediately at the disposal of the Supreme Government from whom they may expect clemency after some considerations are taken up.**
>
> **God and Liberty!**

In other words, Santa Anna would accept nothing less than unconditional surrender.

As the Alamo gate swung open to admit Jameson, Captain Albert Martin emerged. Travis, upset that Bowie had not consulted with him before offering a truce, sent Martin to make it even.

Martin met the smooth talking, New Orleans educated, Colonel Juan Almonte at the footbridge near Potrero Street.

"I am speaking for Colonel William Barret Travis," he said in a clear, steady voice. "If the Colonel [Almonte] wishes to talk things over, he will be received with great pleasure."

Almonte turned to one of his soldiers, laughed, then back to Martin.

"It does not become the Mexican government," he turned his tone serious, "to make any proposition through me. Your only hope is to surrender. If you lay down your arms and promise never to aim them at a Mexican soldier, your lives and property will be spared. Otherwise…"

He stretched a forefinger under his chin and across his neck from ear to ear.

"Is that your answer, Colonel?"

"Si!"

"If Colonel Travis agrees to these terms, I will return with him. Otherwise, we will presume fire."

Thirty minutes later, the 18-pounder thundered Travis' decision.

That evening Santa Anna sat at his desk in the Yturri house, situated on the northwest corner of the Main Plaza, pouring over plans for organizing the siege. It wasn't much of a headquarters, bit it was strong. And would protect him from enemy fire.

Also that evening, José María "Gregorio" Esparza and his family gathered a few belongings and crept off into the dusk.

Silently fording the San Antonio River he, with his wife and four children, trudged up to the southeast side of the Alamo.

A window in the chapel opened and they were lifted in one by one.

Gregorio, apparently recognized as one of Captain Juan Seguín's men, was well versed in the use of artillery and would add strength to their defense.

In 1914, at the age of 86, Gregorio's eldest son, Enrique, gave us this recounting of their entry.

He was then a bright boy of eight:

"It was twilight when we got to the Alamo, and it grew pitch-dark soon afterward. All of the doors were closed and barred. The sentinels that had been on duty without were first called inside and the opening closed. Some sentinels were posted upon the roof, but these were protected by the walls of the Alamo church and the old convent building. We went into the church portion. It was shut up when we arrived. We were admitted through a small window.

"I distinctly remember that I climbed through the window and over a cannon that was placed inside of the church immediately behind the windows. There were several cannon there. Some were back of the doors. Some had been mounted on the roof and some had been placed in the convent. The window was opened to permit us to enter, and it was closed immediately after we got inside."

A few years before this, he told the ***San Antonio Daily Express***: "...Both men and women fell within the walls ...Even children died there...The days were long, and filled with terror...Crockett seemed to be the leading spirit. He was everywhere. Travis was in command, but he depended more upon the judgment of Crockett than on his own..."

In the west wall headquarters, Bowie and Travis were in a heated argument.

"Damn it, Bowie! Why did you send Jameson out without telling me? I thought we had an agreement!"

"Why did you fire that damn cannon? Twice! If there was any chance for negotiation..."

"There never was a chance, Colonel Bowie! And you know it!"

Bowie coughed and reached for his handkerchief. Blood speckled his lips. His knees folded and he collapsed to the floor. For weeks heavy whiskey had kept him going. Now exhaustion allowed for the consumption to take hold.

All formality and hostility forgotten, Travis pushed from behind his desk and crouched beside Bowie's still figure.

Whatever their differences, they were in this together.

"Jim!"

Bowie was barely conscious.

Travis pulled him to a sitting position then, draping an arm over his shoulder, urged him to his feet.

Struggling with the pressingly dead weight, he lowered Bowie to his own cot.

"Spend the night here, Jim. If you're not better by morning, I'll have Dr. Pollard [13] look at you."

Bowie mumbled something too incoherent for Travis to understand.

Next morning Bowie was conscious and coherent, yet too weak to move. Dr. Pollard diagnosed pneumonia.

A litter was brought in and he was conveyed to one of the small rooms in the Low Barracks. As the men carried him off, Juana reached out a supplicant hand, tears distorting her pretty features. She had already lost Ursula. What would happen to her if she also lost Jamie?"

Bowie took the hand with a gentle squeeze.

Turning weakly to Travis, he said, "It's all yours now, Buck. Do the best you can."

It was February 24th.

The first day of the battle.

Early that afternoon, the Mexicans opened fire. Shells rained within the Alamo walls. Men darted for their posts, dodging flying dirt and stones.

Almeron Dickinson climbed to the chapel roof, determined to answer with his own artillery, but thought better of it. They needed to conserve ammunition, and his guns were too small to effectively daunt the enemy at such a distance.

William Carey, on the southwest wall, boomed the 18-pounder.

David Crockett. with his Tennesseans, made his way to the southeast palisade. Rifles blazed and cracked.

Suddenly, the 18-pounder was sent spinning. On another wall, a 12-pounder dislodged.

Huddled in the dark little rooms, the women and children waited with uncertainty for the unearthly noise to cease.

Then, silence.

Darkness had fallen over the land.

The defenders took stock. No one had been killed, or even injured.

Only one horse was slightly wounded.

Travis sat at his desk, his active pen poised above paper.

His men did well this afternoon. They made him proud. Still, how long could they persist? Surely, Santa Anna was holding back, playing a sadistic little game. He'd asked for reinforcements. Yet, received none. Why? Don't they know how crucial this little fortress is to the safety of Texas, and to all the American people?

Commandancy of the Alamo
Bajar, Feby 24th, 1836

To the People of Texas & All Americans in the world —

Fellow citizens & Compatriots — I am besieged by a thousand or more of the Mexicans under Santa Anna — I have sustained a continual bombardment & cannonade for 12 hours [14] **& have not lost a man — The enemy has demanded a surrender at discretion, otherwise, the garrison will be put to the sword, if the fort is taken — I have answered them with a cannon shot, & our flag still waves proudly from the walls — I shall never surrender or retreat. Then, I call on you in the name of liberty, of patriotism & everything dear to the American character, to come to our aid, with all dispatch — The enemy is receiving reinforcements daily & will no doubt increase to three or four thousand in four or five days. If this call is neglected, I am determined to sustain myself as long as possible & die like a soldier who never forgets what is due to his own honor & that of his country — Victory or Death!**

[signed] **William Barret Travis**
Lt. Col. Comdt.

He folded the paper, then opened it and struck three lines under "Victory or Death!"

He refolded the paper, then unfolded it again and wrote a brief, enlightening postscript:

PS. The lord is on our side — When the enemy appeared in sight, we had not three bushels of corn — We have since found, in

deserted houses, 80 or 90 bushels of corn & got into the walls 20 or 30 heads of beeves.

Albert Martin waited patiently while Travis, he decided, worked on his masterpiece. He had been called to deliver an important message to his hometown of Gonzales almost an hour ago. Since then, Travis had torn up two papers, and scratched his head over the one he was handing him now.

Through the open Alamo main gate flew Martin. Past the startled Mexican sentries, south along the irrigation ditch surrounding the fort, then east onto the Gonzales road.

Throughout the silent night, he traveled.

By morning, distant rumblings pierced his ears. Another attack! Lashing his horse, he galloped harder; his poor animal, lathered to froth, pounded dirt with tired legs.

By late afternoon, he reached the Guadalupe River and crossed over to Gonzales.

After talking with Dr. Sutherland, who chose to remain in Gonzales, and rousing thirty-two willing men under a George Kimble of Dickinson and Kimble Hat Factory, Martin handed Travis' dispatch to a Lancelot Smither.

"Relay it as far and as wide as you can," he said, scribbling 'Hurry all the men you can' on its back.

Smither understood, adding a few more words of plea.

Although he was unable to journey further than his home in San Felipe, he would make sure it was passed on.

From the excited town of San Felipe, couriers took copies of it north to Washington-on-the-Brazos (Texas' new capital), east to Nacogdoches, south to Columbia on the Gulf coast.

From Columbia, coastal schooners relayed it to the cotton ports of Galveston, Mobile, Pensacola, New Orleans.

A Mississippi steamer carried it from New Orleans, for chugging east by railway.

By March 30th, it was in New York City. The ***Evening Post*** headlined **LATE FROM TEXAS** above Travis' appeal.

Washington City learned of it the following day. The Whigs, in their seditious paper ***National Intelligencer***, gloated. If President Jackson sent "responsive forces," he could ruin any chance of negotiating purchase of Texas from Mexico. On the other hand, if he sat tight the American people themselves would be "up in arms" against his administration.

Jackson chose to sit tight, inviting the new Mexican minister, Don Eduardo de Gorestiza, for a talk the next day.

It was April 1, 1836. Twenty-six days too late!

In the gray, drizzling dawn of February 25th, the garrison spotted an earthwork going up on their side of the river.

Around 10 a.m., Mexican bugles blared. Cannon blasted. Small figures swarmed across the river, darting for cover among a cluster of adobe and wooden huts and shacks, seen in Spanish occupied days as La Villita. The defenders held fire. Closer, the enemy came. 200 yards… 100…

At 90 yards, the Mexicans charged the Alamo's south wall. The defenders still held fire until they were within point-blank range, then opened up with a barrage of canister, grapeshot, and long rifles.

"David Crockett was seen at all points," wrote Travis in his revealing diary[15], "animating the men to do their duty."

The Mexicans fell back to the shacks and huts, dragging their dead and wounded.

The Alamo gate swung open.

La Villita offered excellent shelter and was dangerously close to the fort.

James Rose with five others emerged carrying torches and, racing forward, enemy lead streaking by on every side, they fired the nearest buildings.

As smoke billowed from thatched roofs, old wood cracked and crumbled. Concealed occupants screamed as flames engulfed everything, while cannon and small arms fire poured down from the Alamo walls.

Once again, there were no Americans down, and the Mexicans had lost most of their cover.

By noon General Ramirez Sesma withdrew his few remaining troops, which had numbered close to 300 when the skirmish began, back to the river in confusion, dragging along his casualties.

At his headquarters, Santa Anna measured the morning's

outcome. This would take longer than he thought.

"Oh, well," he must have told himself. "At least we're on their side of the river. It will be only a matter of surrounding the mission and moving in."

Calling for Colonel Juan Bringas, he sent him to the Rio Grande with orders to fetch General Antonio Gaona and his three best companies. By forced march, if necessary.

Next, he summoned General Sesma.

Sesma entered the little room meekly expecting an upbraiding for his defeat.

"Relax, General," said Santa Anna.

"But I lost..."

"It matters little. It was only the first encounter."

"And our men..."

"They do not concern me," he waved his hand in dismisssal.

Sesma eyed His Excellency with displeasure, remembering a remark he had once heard: "If I were God, I would wish to be more."

Santa Anna did not see the look. He had stepped over to his desk and was studying a map one of his engineers had drawn of the battlefield.

Sesma walked over to the desk.

"When your rear echelons get here, General..."

"They have been coming in all day, mi General."

"Good! Put them to work! I want that entire mission surrounded." (His index finger circled the lines depicting the Alamo.) "I want artillery placed here." (His finger moved south to the river.) "And here." (Up near the southeast wall, the powder house.) "I want our encirclement to be tight!" (He clenched his fist.) "No more of those infernal messengers must leave that place!" (He stabbed the map with his finger,) "Do you understand?"

"I understand."

"Are my instructions clear, General?"

"Si, mi General."

At 9 p.m. a great norther blew up, followed by drenching rain.

In the Alamo, the defenders heard scraping shovels as trenches were dug near the destroyed houses of La Villita.

Working and cursing in the storm, the Mexicans drew as close to the fort as they dared, then looped it in a ring.

The defenders were up to the challenge. Travis fired a 12-pounder, scattering Mexicans for cover. David's long rifle picked off several of the enemy in succession. Twelve of the garrison sallied out for a tussle with some of Sesma's men. Others raided La Villita itself; yanking down more shacks and burning huts bordering the new Mexican earthworks, then spurt back to the Alamo gate.

Balls whizzed from Mexican muskets.

No one was hit.

"Diablos!"

Useless muskets struck the ground in frustration.

During the fighting, several local defenders slipped out

to give themselves up. They were Mexican. Why should they die with these crazy Anglo-Americans?

They asked to speak with Santa Anna, but were told His Excellency had gone to bed and was not to be disturbed.

With the enemy closing in on all sides, the gravity of the situation was increasing.

Travis anxiously dashed off another appeal for help.

This time, to Sam Houston himself:

> **Do hasten aid to me as rapidly as possible, as from the superior number of the enemy it will be impossible for us to keep them out much longer. If they overpower us, we fall a sacrifice at the shrine of our country, and we hope posterity and our country will do our memory justice. Give us help, oh my country.**

Who could he send out? They were completely surrounded

David offered a name. Captain Juan Seguín.

"He's Mexican. An' he speaks it, too."

"No, Crockett. I need him here," insisted Travis.

"Wal, let's take it t' a vote."

"Damn it! We're a long way from Congress, Crockett!"

Travis lowered his head and studied the crude carvings on his old desk. Someone loved Margaret in 1805. Where did this piece of furniture come from?

"But," Travis smiled at a rough scratching of a Spanish officer receiving a kick in the pants by a Mexican soldier, "since no one has a mind to go, anyway…"

Seguin was overwhelmingly elected courier.

"Damn!" Travis shook his head at a grinning David Crockett. "I'd make one hell of a lousy politician."

Crossing to the Low Barracks, Seguin asked Jim Bowie if he could borrow his horse.

Tossing with fever, Bowie was at first unable to recognize him or understand what was said. Finally, he did. Yes, of course you may borrow my horse. But, take care of it. I'll need it soon.

Seguín and his orderly, Antonio Cruz, rode out into the rain-swept night, turning east for the Gonzales road.

Challenged by a guard of dragoons, Seguin hollered in Spanish that they were friends — good Mexicans — and casually approached the outpost.

Suddenly, the horsemen spurred left, racing past the startled sentries.

Shouts… Shots… And a mad scramble for horses.

The frightened animals pulled away from their stumbling owners, making it impossible for them to mount.

Some of the horses managed to give chase… Rider less.

By the time everything was untangled, Seguín and Cruz were well on their way.

Unknown to Travis, relief readied to move toward the Alamo.

On the afternoon of February 26th, Colonel Fannin, with

320 men and four cannon, marched out of Goliard.

Meanwhile, Travis was not idle.

He sent a detachment to tear down more of the La Villita shacks for wood to help heat the Alamo's now frigid interior, another to scoop buckets of water from an irrigation ditch west of the fort, still another — after dark — to burn the remaining huts providing enemy shelter.

On the Alamo walls, riflemen were kept busy. Whenever an unfortunate Mexican soldier popped up his head, it jerked back to the ground. Usually, each man kept four or five loaded rifles by his side; and his aim was deadly.

David roamed from palisade to wall. When Ol' Betsy roared, a Mexican dropped.

Climbing to the southwest corner, he spotted an unlucky officer inspecting his men some 200 yards away. Coolly leveling his rifle, he shot the man dead.

February 27th, found the defenders facing a new peril. Mexican troops, well out of range of even David's long rifle, were blocking irrigation in an attempt to cut off the fort's water supply.

To quell this, Green Jameson ardently put his men to work finishing a well started on the corral end of the plaza.

Digging four feet further down they hit water, yet collapsed a mound of earth and timber inside the cattle pen.

With the loss of this parapet, it would be difficult, if not impossible, to fire safely within that enclosure.

On February 28th, Jim Bowie asked to have his cot taken out to the plaza.

Though still desperately ill, he urged the men to keep up the fight.

"...And cheer up," he said to downcast faces. "All is not lost, yet."

These words were of little comfort. Though food supplies were adequate for the moment, with little rest or sleep they had little reason to feel cheerful.

"Let's have us some fun," he insisted, raising himself partially from his cot. "Crockett, break out your fiddle. McGregor, go get your bagpipes."

From the day they met, David would challenge McGregor to see who could make the most noise.

Today, they took turns — David scratching, McGregor blowing — while the garrison hooted, whooped and laughed. For a time they forgot. They forgot the hopelessness; and the loneliness hopelessness brings.

The previous night, Santa Anna had sent a glowing dispatch to Mexico City, reporting his triumphant capture of San Antonio de Béxar.

He failed to mention, however, that a small band of rag-tag Texas rebels stood across the river in defiance of over a thousand well-equipped, well-trained Mexican troops.

Two hundred yards out of Goliard, Fannin ran into trouble. A supply wagon broke down. Further on, two more of the wooden oxcarts fell apart. Delays for repairs took hours.

To make matters worse; while the men rested overnight some of the oxen wandered off into the north wind.

Discouraged, Fannin elected to suspend the Alamo rescue and return his men to Ft. Defiance. Travis and Bowie would have to fend for themselves.

Fifty miles southwest of Goliard, General José de Urrea surprised Colonel Frank Johnson and 50 of his remaining Matamoros expedition at San Patricio.

Though Johnson and four of his little group managed to escape, the rest were slaughtered.

Captain John Stover Brooks, an aide to Colonel Fannin, would write to his family of the incident on February 29th:

> **General Urrea put the whole garrison under the command of Col. Frank Johnson to the sword. Five of them reached this place, and are probably all that have escaped. Captain Pearson of the volunteers, was killed with several others, after they had surrendered. The war is to be one of extermination. Each party seems to understand that no quarters are to be given or asked.**

Throughout the past five days, Santa Anna had filled every night with bugle calls, jeers, bursts of artillery and volleys of musketry.

By Monday, February 29th, the garrison was worn-down and jittery from lack of sleep. Even David Crockett had lost some of his usual cheerfulness. Yet, they hung on. Perhaps they found themselves bound by a common agent. Perhaps they still believed Travis' extensive messages would rouse the rest of Texas from its lethargy. Or perhaps they felt, if no one else cared, they were making a lone stand for freedom.

At 3 a.m., Tuesday, March 1st, a cold and tired Alamo sentry heard movement in the brush below the north wall and fired through a heavy rain.

"Damn your stupid ass, anyhow," came a muffled curse from the dark.

American!

Quickly, the watchman called down to the men guarding the postern:

"Americans! Open the gate!"

Albert Martin made a dash for the slim light as the gate opened a crack, with John W. Smith and 32 Gonzales men following, one limping beside his horse.

"Who's th' bastard what shot me in th' foot?"

That morning, David grabbed for his fiddle. McGregor snatched his bagpipes. They were celebrating the first sign of hope since the siege began. Texas was waking up.

Even Buck Travis joined in the festivities in his own way.

Apparently in a fit of whimsy, he sent one of Dickinson's artillerymen to the 12-pounder aimed over the west wall. A double blast flew at a lively little house on the Main Plaza. One ball missed, but the second slammed into the building, sending stone, timber, and Mexican soldiers soaring. They had just hit Santa Anna's headquarters.

Unfortunately, His Excellency was out inspecting one of his camps, some 800 yards north.

Eight hundred yards to the north, Santa Anna scampered for cover at the sound of an explosion. Then, realizing he was in no danger, got up, dusted his uniform and straightened his hat.

Gradually regaining his somewhat ruptured dignity, he looked around for any sign of mirth. He saw none. Good! They would have been instantly shot if he had!

"Dig more trenches!" he ordered Colonel Pedro de Ampudia.

Ampudia saluted, a deadpan expression on his face.

Mounting his horse, Santa Anna loftily pranced back to the Main Plaza.

He was out of earshot when outbursts of laughter erupted

from his troops.

Wearily dismounting, Santa Anna went into the Yturri house to inspect its damage.

His soldiers were busily clearing away the wreckage.

He smiled.

At least his office hadn't sustained much destruction. Excellent! If need be, he'd hold up behind this stout screening until his army annihilated the last wretched rebel in that old mission they called a fort.

In Washington-on-the-Brazos, delegates gathered to vote for independence.

The date was March 1, 1836.

On March 2, 1836, Texas' Declaration of Independence passed through the convention. A lone star flag symbolically waved her release [16].

In the Alamo, though, Washington-on-the-Brazos was a world away. When March 2nd came with no trace of Fannin, the garrison resigned themselves to a certainty that no further help could be expected. Even Jim Bonham, sent out on February 16th, to guide Fannin personally into Béxar, seemingly let them down.

James Butler Bonham, considered by Travis his most cogent persuader, was born near Red Bank, South Carolina on February 20, 1807. By 1830, he was a lawyer practicing in

Pendleton, South Carolina. Five years later he was in Texas, talking directly to Sam Houston. Within two weeks, he was a lieutenant in the Texas cavalry. "His influence in the army is great," wrote Houston in his recommendation to promote Bonham to major. "More so than some who would be generals."

From the day Bonham first left for Goliard, Travis began marking time. He should have reached Fannin by February 18th. Where is he? Perhaps he didn't make it through.

Although he had not believed Colonel Bowie's prediction that Santa Anna would march through winter, Travis' idea was to show force when the Mexican dictator finally invaded the town. He had hoped for a repeat of the victorious siege of Béxar.

Bonham did indeed reach Goliard on February 18th, but discovered Fannin unwilling to attempt a march to Béxar. He would not make a move without orders from General Houston, he told the surprised courier. Besides, Ft. Defiance needed to prepare for its own defense. He would wait. Goliard should not be left unattended.

"Stay here," urged Fannin. "Béxar is ill-fated."

"No! I promised Colonel Travis that I would get help."

Galloping for Gonzales, he stopped at Victoria and several towns along the way without successfully raising interest.

When he finally arrived in Gonzales he found it empty, save for the women and children. Its younger men were headed toward the Alamo, while its seniors were convoked to Washington-on-the-Brazos.

On March 1st, 19-year-old Benjamin Franklin Highsmith sped into Gonzales.

Pouring out his close call with the enemy on Powder House Hill, he pleaded for Bonham not to return to the hapless fort.

Highsmith had been one of the first messengers to leave Béxar with an appeal for Fannin. Having been turned down, he was returning alone when spotted by the Mexican cavalry and chased for six miles.

"No one can get through the Mexican lines. Stay here!" the young man begged.

Instead, saddling his horse the next morning, Bonham forded the Guadalupe River.

"I will report the result of my mission to Colonel Travis, or die in the attempt," he had stubbornly told Highsmith.

In his saddlebag he bore a letter from Robert M, "Three-Legged Willie" Williamson, a major in the newly-formed Texas Rangers, assuring Travis that help was on the way and urging him to hold out.

Although it appeared encouraging on the surface, this letter did not ring entirely true. Bonham felt it was Williamson's bid to pacify. He would let Colonel Travis decide.

From the top of Powder House Hill, he studied the Alamo less than a mile away. Mexican camps surrounded her on all four sides. Mounted earthworks, smoky fires, troops and cavalry encircled the place. Highsmith was right. Breaking through seemed impossible.

"Impossible," however, was not in Jim Bonham's vocabulary.

Veering to his right, he quietly worked his way east through the brush and thickets. At a point — as near as he could judge — between two enemy lines, he spurred out of the bushes, pounding straight for the corral gate.

Hunching low on his horse, he hurled safely into the Alamo. It was 11 a.m., March 3rd. The stunned Mexicans, never expecting anyone to enter the doomed mission, fired errant and erratic volleys.

Travis dismissed Williamson's letter, shoving it wrinkled into his pocket. It just didn't make sense. With all the entreaties he had sent out, reinforcements would have been here by now.

Still, he was an eternal optimist when confronted by any form of subjection. There was yet hope, he would have thought. Help might come from San Felipe, Brazoria, or from a dozen other towns.

Near 11:55 a.m., loud shouts reached the Alamo walls. Had the garrison's hopes been answered?

Expectantly rushing to the parapets, the gun platforms, the chapel top, they stared forlornly into the glare of a noonday sun.

Over a thousand Mexican soldiers paraded in from the west. General Gaona's brigades had arrived from the Rio Grande. Santa Anna now had 2,400 crack troops to 191 weary defenders.

At 11: 45 p.m. that night, John W. Smith saddled up for another attempt to rouse aid for the besieged garrison.

When word spread that he was going, Private Willis Albert Moore of Mississippi handed Smith a note to his family.

Others did the same.

They now knew their fate.

In his west wall headquarters, Travis formed what he believed would be his last appeal:

> **The power of Santa Anna is to be met here or in the colonies; we had better meet them here than to suffer a war of devastation to rage on our settlements. A blood-red banner waves from the church of Béxar, & in the camp above us** [17]**, in token that the war is one of vengeance against rebels; they have declared us as such; demanded that we should surrender at discretion, or that this garrison should be put to the sword. Their threats have no influence on me or my men, but to make all fight with desperation & that high-souled courage that characterizes the patriot, who is willing to die in defense of his country's liberty & his own honor.**

It was addressed to "Richard Ellis, President, Washington-on-Brazos."

Turning to his own personal messages he wrote to Rebecca Cummings, a young Texas beauty he had hoped to marry once his divorce from Rosanna finalized. Caressing a lock of her hair, he penned shaky lines of a lover's last farewell. Then, gently kissing her tress, he placed it carefully back into his breast pocket.

Next, he jotted a letter to his friend, Jesse Grimes:

> **Let the convention go on & make a declaration of independence, & we will understand & the world will understand, what we are fighting for. If independence is not declared** [18]**, I shall lay down my arms, & so will the men under my command. But under the flag of independence, we are ready to peril our lives a hundred times a day.**

His eyes moistened as he fastened upon a torn sheet of yellow wrapping paper. "Take care of my little boy, " he wrote to David Ayers, who was boarding his son Charles [19] near Washington-on-the-Bazos. "If the country should be saved, I will make him a splendid fortune; but if the country should be lost & I should perish, he will have nothing but the recollections that he is the son of a man who died for his country."

Solemnly, Travis delivered his packet of letters to Smith. Then, remembering something he forgot to put in the official dispatch to Ellis, said:

"Tell the reinforcement to bring ten days' rations.

Smith nodded, mounting his horse.

"Oh, and Smitty, be sure to emphasize that we'll need at least 500 pounds of cannon powder, 200 pounds of balls for our 6, 12 and 18-pounders, and 10 kegs of rifle powder. I've listed them, but be sure you make it clear that we need them."

Another afterthought.

"I'll fire the 18-pounder three times a day, morning, noon and night, to let everyone know that the Alamo still stands."

Again Smith nodded, trotting for the south gate. Eager to be off.

The northern gate opened. A dozen defenders charged out to distract the enemy with random fire. Mexican patrols from the south and east rushed to the scene. Guns blazed on both sides.

The south gate swung open. Smith galloped through, turned east, and vanished into darkness.

March 4th brought cannon fire on the north. Earth and stone spewed the plaza from a smashed north wall. Jameson and his men frantically tried to shore up its gaping breach, piling rubble back into place.

Sesma's howitzers hammered the west wall.

From every sector bombs hurled in, shattering and destroying.

Bolting for the southeast palisade to join his "boys," David aimed his rifle. At what? All he could see was artillery.

In another rare moment of discouragement, he patted Ol' Betsy and repeated words he had spoken to Susanna Dickinson a few days earlier: "I think we'd better march out an' die in th' open air. I don't like bein' hemmed in."

During the bombardment, more Tejanos — taking advantage of an amnesty offer announced earlier in the day — deserted the Alamo. It seemed likely Santa Anna would win. And to be on the losing side of His Excellency meant... So Rodriguez, Flores, Garza and Silvero scrambled to safety.

That evening, Trinidad Saucedo slipped out of the fortress and made her way across the river to the Yturri house.

Though readying for bed Santa Anna heedfully listened to the information she seemed unable to contain. The Anglo-Americans are in distress, she said. Their defenses are crumbling. The men are weak. Their ammunition is low. The place can easily be taken.

"Excellent!" he smiled, handing the young woman a coin and dismissing her with a wave.

"Tomorrow, we shall prepare for the final assault," he said to one of his guards, who stared straight ahead.

Saturday morning, March 5th, awakened to heavier blasts from enemy cannon. During the night, Mexican artillery had pushed within 200 yards of the fort. Defenders darted for whatever protection they could find. Brisk fire pounded crumbling walls.

According to Travis' diary, "David Crockett was seen in

every section of the fort." Leveling Ol' Betsy here, aiming her there. With nearly each shot, a Mexican fell. Taking his favorite position on the southwest wall, he began picking targets.

Major Raphael Soldana (a captain in the Tampico Battalion during the battle) later signed an affidavit describing a sharpshooter firing from this parapet:

> **A tall man, with flowing hair, was seen firing from the same place on the parapet during the entire siege.**
>
> **He wore a buckskin suit and cap all of a pattern entirely different from those worn by his comrades.**
>
> **This man would kneel or lie down behind the low parapet, rest his long gun and fire, and we all learned to keep at a good distance when he was seen to make ready to shoot. He rarely missed his mark, and when he fired he always rose to his feet and calmly reloaded his gun, seemingly indifferent to the shots fired by our men.**
>
> **He had a strong, resonant voice and often railed at us, but as we did not understand English we could not comprehend the import of his words further than they were defiant.**
>
> **This man I later learned was known as "Kwockey."**

By late afternoon, March 5th, Mexican fire tapered off, then ceased.

Around 5 p.m., Travis summoned his garrison to assemble in the plaza.

Jim Bowie was hauled out on his cot.

Susanna Dickinson leaned against a near building, pensively watching the spent men shuffle over.

"My brave companions," Travis' voice wavered. He was as drained as his men. "We are overwhelmed. Our fate is sealed. Within a few days, perhaps within a few hours, we must all be in eternity. This is our destiny and we cannot avoid it.

"I have deceived you long by my promise of help. But I crave your pardon. For, in deceiving you, I also deceived myself, having been first deceived by others. Colonel Fannin and Texas have failed you."

He took a deep breath to regain his composure.

"It is no longer a question of how we may save our lives, but how best to prepare for death.

"If we surrender, we will be shot without taking the life of a single one of our enemy. If we try to make our escape, we shall be butchered before we can dispatch our adversaries. To either of these courses I am opposed, and I ask you to withstand the advance of the enemy."

Travis became animated. Words he thought he no longer had the strength to deliver, gushed forth:

"When they shall storm the fort and scale our walls at last, let us slay them as they come! As they leap over the ramparts, slay we all of them until our arms are powerless to lift our weapons in defense of ourselves!"

Drawing his sword, he observed each grave face before him. Then, regrettably, he looked down at Bowie lying weak, pale, emaciated.

"Yet to every man I give permission to surrender or attempt to escape. My desire and decision is to remain in the fort and fight as long as breath remains in my body. But do as you think best, each of you."

Scratching a line in the dirt, his sword easily embedding its mark, he called on the defenders to take their position:

"Those who will remain and fight until we die, step across this line."

A Young, less wearied, Tapley Holland, 26-year-old son of a War of 1812 veteran, stepped proudly abreast his commander.

David Crockett whispered to his rifle, "Wal, Betsy ol' gal, 'pears we got us some work t' do."

Stroking her length with the tenderness of a loving husband, he strolled over beside Holland.

His "Tennessee boys" followed.

Then, Captain Almeron Dickinson and his crew.

Jim Bonham.

One by one, and in groups, they tramped over until only two remained; a standing man, with one too weak to move.

"Boys," rasped Bowie. "I'm not able to come to you, but I wish some of you would be so kind as to remove my cot over there."

He raised a frail, trembling finger and pointed to a spot next to Travis.

Four men ran over, grasped his cot, and scurried him across.

The standing man remained anchored. He was Louis "Moses" Rose.

Rose claimed to have been a soldier in the Napoléonic Wars, having marched with Bonaparte "all the way to Moscow."

Historical records show this to be true. However, one thing is also certain. Rose was an illiterate mercenary who fought, not for patriotic ideals that move individuals to the ultimate sacrifice, but for pay and plunder. And, like most mercenaries when defeat appears imminent, they leave the scene.

Within ten minutes Rose was out of the fort, and out of heroic history. Though making good his escape, he would be labeled a coward for the rest of his life [20].

With John W. Smith still traveling for help — and Louis Rose fleeing over the wall — the defenders numbered a little over 185.

Of the noncombatants, there remained 26 women and children.

Travis' Negro slave Joe considered himself a garrison member, yet fired no more than a single shot throughout the siege. Technically he, too, was a noncombatant [21].

As Trinidad Saucedo left his headquarters on March 4th, Santa Anna ordered an immediate council of war. This was unusual for him, since he never asked for anyone's advice.

Generals, colonels, and a major filed into the room. Why

were they called out so abruptly? What was so important?

"Gentlemen," began Santa Anna, pacing the floor in back of his desk. "The time has come to take the Alamo!"

"I do not agree, mi General," said Cos, opening a debate.

Santa Anna seated himself and leaned back in his chair, woefully listening to his brother-in-laws latest prattle. Now he knew why he detested conferences.

"Our artillery is not yet strong enough to completely penetrate the Alamo walls," whined Cos. "Why not wait for General Gaona's two 12-pounders? They should be here any day…"

"I agree with General Cos," broke in General Manuel Fernández Castrillón, an old veteran of the Spanish occupation, turning restlessly in his seat, "The cannon should be up from the Rio Grande on the 7th. Why not wait?"

Colonel José María Romero nodded approval of Cos' and Castrillón's suggestion.

"No! No! No!" shouted Colonel Almonte. "I agree with His Excellency. We should attack NOW!"

Sesma, wishing vindication for his La Villita defeat, sided with Almonte.

Colonel Francisco Duque and Colonel Agustín Amat were unable to make a decision either way.

The one major, who wondered what he was doing there at all, chose a tactful silence.

Hearing enough, Santa Anna stood up.

"Then it's settled, gentlemen. Tomorrow, we prepare for the final assault.

The officers stood and filed out; some disgruntled, some elated, one confused.

Santa Anna tiredly lowered to his seat.

Opening one of the drawers in his desk, he pulled out a little brown bottle and pried the cork stopper from its wide mouth with a penknife. Carefully measuring snow-white powder onto the knife, he placed a small portion on his tongue, washed it down with a sip of wine, and sat back to await regeneration.

The bottle's label pictured a skull and crossbones. Above it were impressed the words: ***Sulfate of Morphine***.

By two o'clock on the afternoon of March 5th, Santa Anna's plans were complete.

The assault would begin at 4 p.m., March 6th. Four columns would strike the Alamo simultaneously. General Cos would attack the northwest corner… Colonel Duque, the northeast… Colonel Romero, the east… Colonel Juan Morales, the southeast palisade.

General Sesma's cavalry would patrol all sides; with orders to cut down any rebels or soldanos attempting to flee.

Santa Anna himself would command the new battery north of the fortress.

Counting Sesma's cavalry, the entire assault force consisted of 1,800 men; about three-fourths of Santa Anna's army. The rest — mostly convicts and inexperienced recruits — were kept in reserve in Béxar and at the new battery.

Around two-thirty that afternoon couriers sped from post to post, dispatching copies of Santa Anna's orders.

Everything was laid out in minutest detail:

> **The troops under Cos must carry 10 scaling ladders, 2 crowbars, 2 axes.**
>
> **All chinstraps must be down.**
>
> **All arms must be in perfect working condition. Their bayonets sharp!**

By 7 p.m., the first Mexican troops stacked their weapons and bedded down for a little sleep.

By 10 p.m., the last Mexican cannon ceased firing.

By 10: 30 p.m., an oppressive silence loomed heavy over the lines.

And in this ominous stillness, murmurings prayed for eternal souls.

Captain José Juan Sánchez Navarro, General Cos' able adjutant, took out his diary and scratched by match light:

> **Why is it that Santa Anna always wants to mark his triumphs with blood and tears?**

As clouds blanketed the moon, Colonel Travis quietly woke 16-year-old James L. Allen. He had one more desperate appeal to Fannin.

Riding bareback, Allen urgently tore out of the south exit, through the Mexican lines, and on to Goliard.

"We have heard from Bexar," wrote Captain Brooks on

the morning of March 9th. "It is feared that the Alamo will be taken, and that all the devoted courage of the brave defenders will be of no avail."

In the Alamo chapel, Travis removed a gold cat's-eye ring, thread it on a string, then looped it around the neck of 15-month-old Angelina Dickinson. The ring had been a gift from Rebecca Cummings. He had no further use of it.

At the southeast palisade, David Crockett told a last joke before closing his eyes in sleep.

Most of the garrison settled down for a few hours' rest.

In the Low Barracks, Jim Bowie tossed with fever.

On the north wall, Adjutant John Baugh, officer of the day, stood watch.

Near 4 a.m., Travis returned to his headquarters in the west wall, placed his sword and double-barreled shotgun by the side of his cot, and wrapped himself in a blanket against the morning chill. On the floor beside him slumbered 23-year-old Joe.

The hour of attack — 4 a.m. — came and went. Santa Anna had decided to postpone the assault until there was sufficient light.

Just after 5 a.m. his troops, having been awakened at midnight to lie in readiness in the cold grass, could contain themselves no longer. From somewhere, a cry went up: "Viva Santa Anna…Viva la Republic!" Followed by shouts and cheers from every column.

Santa Anna had hoped for a surprise attack. This was no longer possible.

He gave the signal.

Bugles sounded. ***Deguello* — the song of death!** No quarter! No mercy!

"Ariba!" shouted Cos to his men lying barely 200 yards from the fort.

Jumping to their feet, they grabbed their ladders, crowbars and axes, and surged maniacally toward the north wall.

Bugle calls, shouts and yells came from every direction as column after column charged the Alamo.

On the north wall, John Baugh was startled. The sentries posted outside the walls gave no warning, yet the Mexicans were here. Everywhere!

Racing for the barracks, Baugh bellowed for all to hear: "Colonel Travis! The Mexicans are coming!"

Bounding from his cot, Travis buckled on his sword, snatched his shotgun and homespun jacket [22] and, yelling for Joe to grab his pistol and follow, ran across the plaza to the north wall.

Leaping to the battery, he looked around. No enemy could be sighted, but the tumultuous roar below — exploding rockets lighting the shadowy sky above — told him the invasion they had repelled since the siege began [23] was on.

"Come on, boys!" he shouted. "The Mexicans are upon us, and we'll give them hell!"

Almeron Dickinson, Jim Bonham, and Dickinson's crew

scrambled up the ramp to swing into action their three 12-pounders atop the chapel's impaired roof.

David Crockett and his Tennesseans were at the south-east palisade.

"Here they come, boys. Give'em hell!"

David fired. Juan Basquez tumbled forward, his musket slipping from a relaxed hand, a bullet through the brain; the first soldier to die in the final assault.

He had planned a return to his trade as a shoemaker in Durango following his stint in Santa Anna's army. He had nine years to go.

Slinging his jacket over a peg by a cannon, Travis took full command of the north wall battery.

Alive with exhilaration, he urged his men on.

"Hurrah, my boys," he shouted over and over again.

To the Tejano defenders, he called out:

"No rendise, muchachos!" [24]

This is what he had been waiting for all of his short life; to take charge as supreme commander.

Brandishing his sword in one hand, his shotgun in the other, he bustled from cannon to cannon.

"Give them hell boys. Victory or death!"

Suddenly, the top rung of a ladder appeared. Then, another positioned itself. The Mexicans were scaling the wall.

Travis leaned over and fired both barrels into an ascending scattering of men below.

From the darkness, musketry answered. His head jerked back, a tiny bluish tinge dotting his forehead.

Dropping his shotgun among the climbing enemy, he fell backwards against a hot cannon where, attempting to raise himself, he slid into a sitting position and died.

A horrified Joe missed a shot with his pistol and ran for one of the buildings, taking a slight wound with a musket ball as he fled. He was not seen again until after the battle.

In the dark sacristy, Susanna Dickinson clutched little Angelina to her apron. The Mexicans would see her dead before anything happened to her daughter.

Darting into the room, 16-year-old Galba Fuqua of Gonzales desperately tried to tell her something; but a musket ball had shattered his jaw. Blood trickled his lips.

Susanna shook her head. She couldn't understand.

Holding his jaws together with both hands, he struggled for words. Still nothing. Frustrated, he turned and rushed back outside.

Meanwhile, Captain Almeron Dickinson and his artillerymen were busy.

From the chapel roof heavy grape pinned the east and south columns, pressuring them into retreat.

Rifle fire from the southeast palisade hurried them along.

On the northeast Colonel Duque crumpled, his leg shattered. His frantic troops, pitching recklessly forward, trampled his body. He was barely able to drag himself to safety.

Two grapeshot blasts shred Cos' northwest column, tearing away forty men. A few managed to reach the wall —

those fired upon by Travis — but the majority fell back.

Whipping stragglers with the flats of their sabres, the Mexican officers pressed a second advance. However, once more the withering sheets of grape and rifle fire turned them around.

From his vantage point at the new battery, Santa Anna fumed. He expected this to take only a few minutes. It was now almost six-o'clock.

"Almonte!" he called, his eyes blazed with fury and the effects of opium.

"Si, mi General?"

"Regroup! Regroup! Ready the reserves. We will hit the walls to the last man. I want no more retreats! Do you understand? **No more retreats!**"

"Si, mi General. It will be done."

While the Mexicans reformed, David Crockett ran over to Dr. Pollard, who was working alone to staunch the blood of defenders still moving.

"How many dead, Doct'r?"

"I Count thirty-two."

"How many wound'd?"

"Sixty."

"How many o' th' wound'd cin fight?"

"None should. But I think they all will."

"Here they come!" shouted a voice lost to history.

David sprinted to the palisade and leaned his left shoulder against its strong timber, priming Ol' Betsy. He was totally committed to the outcome of the battle. Whatever his dreams of a greater future had been dashed by a tyrant sitting somewhere out of rifle range.

What his thoughts were at this time, we will never know. Perhaps he thought of his wife, his children, the mountains of Tennessee. Or, of "Beautiful Betsy," the rifle he had packed so carefully away for his return, a return that would have brought his family to their new home in Texas.

His only dream now was to die in the manner in which he lived — to yield to no man. Though treasuring life, if survival meant disgrace he would choose death.

Bugles blared. The band struck ***Deguello***'s bloodcurdling chords. For the Moorish wars in ancient Spain, it announced: "to cut the throat." For Santa Anna, it would be no different.

With a shriek, the troops charged onto the battlefield. Again, Dickinson's artillery and rifles from the southeast palisade stopped Romero's eastern column. Only this time, instead of reverting, they moved to the right, mixing with the Toluca Battalion on the north. Cos' column — halted by the northwest guns — shifted to the left, also merging with Toluca's northern advance. Now, all three columns — in a single bundled body — surged toward the north wall.

Firing blindly ahead, often hitting the backs of their own

men, they finally reached the wall and huddled there for fifteen minutes, not knowing what next to do. They were protected from the immobile cannon, yet were still in danger of rifles firing down from the top. Notwithstanding their vast numbers, Santa Anna's marvelously coordinated army was in serious trouble.

Santa Anna was disconcerted, his peerless ego crushed by the failure of others.

He mounted his horse as if to lead a final charge, then changed his mind.

"Imbeciles," he muttered, dismounting and angrily slapping his horse's rump, which started to run but was caught and held fast by two of Santa Anna's orderlies.

Dropping heavily into his observation chair, he called for Colonel Amat.

"Send in the reserves! Put the Sappers to work."

Next, he summoned Almonte.

"Colonel! Go down there and encourage those idiots to scale that wall, even if you have to shoot some of them to do it! Take my entire staff, including Secretary Caro!"

Although nodding agreement to this order, Almonte did not intend joining the combat at this stage so he, with civilian Secretary Caro, unknown to Santa Anna, personally selected to stay clear of the battlefield.

Left alone with his band and the two orderlies still holding his horse, His Excellency sat back in his chair and lowered his head. He was tired, and a little sad. What would

Napoléon think of a general, with a huge army, who could not even destroy an old mission defended by an insignificant gang of rebels. Napoléon would not think much of this general [25].

Coursing wildly across the harsh ground to the Alamo, the reserves, grenadiers and Zapadores took full impact of the fort's firepower, "falling as grass before a scythe." Bodies rolled over bodies, until the earth underneath was scarcely visible.

Taking advantage of this distraction the Mexicans under the north wall, led by General Juan Amador, looked for a way to breach the fort. The ladders, having been dropped and trampled to kindling underfoot, were of no use.

Coming upon a redoubt hastily built by Jameson to shore up a crumbling section of the wall, Amador clutched one of the jutting timbers. Chinks and uneven beam-ends twined as high as he could see.

"Ariba!" he yelled, pulling himself up. His frenzied men followed.

Up, up they inched, clawing at the rough wood.

With both Texian and Mexican bullets whizzing past, they were frantic. Stomping on each other's hands, they worked their way up until Amador tumbled onto the parapet, they falling beside him.

The Mexicans had entered the Alamo.

Meanwhile, General Cos and his column trailed the west side of the north wall. Embrasures, created by Texian guns firing through, rather than over the wall, invited entry.

Squirming in faster than the defenders could shoot, they opened the northern postern.

An unbridled flow of Mexicans streamed in.

"Great God, Sue," cried Almeron Dickinson, bursting into the sacristy, "the Mexicans are inside our walls!"

He embraced his trembling wife and then he was gone.

His parting words would sound in her ears for years to come:

"If they spare you, save our child."

The 12-pounders turned to the north. The lighter cannon did the same. A shower of grape ripped the enemy ranks.

At the southeast palisade, David and his twelve had repulsed Colonel Morales' column for a bad half-hour. The "weak point" proved anything but.

Pulling his men back, he moved to the southwest corner where they regrouped and climbed a barbette housing the 18-pounder.

Captain William Carey and his gunners, diverted by the action to the north, fell easy prey to an avalanche of slashing bayonets.

The "big gun" was now in Mexican hands.

Descending to the plaza, Morales then charged the south gate from the rear. Other troops assaulted the front. Chaos reigned, as the defenders desperately tried to resist.

"I can tell you," a Mexican soldier would write his brother, "the whole scene was one of extreme terror. After some three-quarters of an hour of the most horrible fire, there followed the most awful attack with hand arms."

Quartermaster Eliel Melton had had enough. Acompanied by a handful of Tejano and Texian defenders, he leaped through a smashed palisade into the silvery dawn, only to be cut to pieces by Sesma's cavalry.

Backed against the Long Barrack's southeast corner, David Crockett and his Tennesseans fought with a fury that awed even their attackers. With rifles emptied, they lashed out at the oncoming enemy with their weapon butts.

Over and over, they clubbed at the high helmets, David flailing Ol' Betsy. However, sheer numbers were taking their toll. When one fell, two resumed his place. When a half-dozen dropped, a dozen seemed to appear. Seven Tennessians went down in a blaze of fire, and under hacking bayonets.

To nearly a man, the southeast defenders were slaughtered as they battled with gun butts, knives, and bare hands. Daniel Cloud kicked and gouged, until his lungs were punctured by bayonet thrusts.

David stood alone, his shoulders rubbing the Long Barrack's course wall.

He was being hemmed in.

Raising Ol' Betsy high, he whacked two heads and then moved forward, swinging right to left, left to right, like a soul possessed. The Mexicans staggered back.

More heads were crushed by heavy strokes.

"Kwocky!" screamed a voice in recognition.

"Venga!" cried another.

Of the hot volley spewed toward the rampaging figure, not one hit its mark. When the smoke cleared, two more helmeted skulls dangled, their bodies crumpling.

"Will you come int' my bow'r [26]," David's grin had never been so wide, his eyes so aglow.

Suddenly, Ol' Betsy cracked, her stock slivering to the bloody muck. Pulling out his hunting knife, he grabbed the nearest Mexican and sank it into the underbelly of a blue and white uniform. There was a low moan. Not of pain, but of surprise. Death itself is painless.

Out of this frenzy, Lieutenant Damasco Martínez whipped his sabre, striking David above the right eye. He fell.

Twenty hungry bayonets then rushed his body.

Each would later claim honor for killing the famous "Kwocky." Yet, it was the young lieutenant who dealt the finishing wound.

David Crockett was dead before touching the ground.

Still, the battle raged on.

Captain John Baugh gave the signal to pull back to the Long Barrack and ran toward the building.

Dropping from the walls, each defender moved for the barrack with grim determination. Taking a few steps, stopping, turning, firing.

Once inside, Baugh and several of the men hurried behind parapets set up for Travis' planned last stand.

These were made of dirt shoved between stretched cowskins; semi circled to effectively block the doorway and positioned high enough to rest a rifle.

Others hastened to rooms where portholes had been hollowed out through walls three feet thick.

Searing fire soon broke from the barrack, frantically scattering the encroaching Mexicans for cover. But in the bare, open plaza, there was no place to hide. Diffused troops fell in heaps in the dawning light.

General Amador, on the north wall, ordered his men to swing one of the cannon around.

Kicking Travis' body from the parapet, they began blasting the Long Barrack's barricaded doorway.

On the southwest wall, Colonel Morales' men pulled the 18-pounder around and took aim. The Long Barrack's barrier flew apart.

While the Mexicans in the plaza took heart and crashed through the smashed entrance, Lieutenant José María Torres of the Zapadores spied something on the roof of the Long Barrack, a strange blue flag fluttering easily in the early morning breeze. A rebel flag!

Unknown to Torres, this was the fine silk banner brought to Texas by the New Orleans Greys militia [27].

Climbing up to the roof, Torres angrily ripped at the reprehensible symbol. Texian bullets whined about him.

Three sergeants from the Jiminéz Battalion lay dead in their attempt to reach the flag.

Pulling down the banner, he replaced it with the red, white and green of Centralist Mexico.

Lieutenant Damasco Martínez, who felled David Crockett earlier in the fighting, had come to help; and died for his trouble. Torres himself was shot as he stuffed the prize inside his tunic.

He would never receive the reward he had hoped for. Santa Anna would never know of his courage.

In the Long Barrack, gleeful Mexicans charged through the destroyed barricade. Now close enough to use their gleaming bayonets, with the defenders unable to reload their rifles, a lust for blood crazed their every move.

Hacking and mutilating, they worked their way from room to room and up to the hospital floor, where the dying offered little resistance.

Down on the first floor, the defenders struggled as best they could by wrestling, kicking and biting their attackers. However, superior odds would again extract their due.

When living Texians were no more, they gored the dead. Ghastly, twisted bodies littered the entire building.

In the Low Barracks, Jim Bowie sat weakly up in his cot, his back braced against a wall, twin pistols beside him, his famous knife on his lap. He was barely strong enough to raise any of the weapons, but would do his best.

Outside the Low Barracks, Morales' men tramped from door to door. Theirs was simply a mopping-up job, with no resistance expected.

Or so they thought…

Pounding into a small room just to the right of the south gate, Sergeant Enrique Alvarez dropped. Then, another fell.

Bowie, with an effort beyond human endurance, had snatched up both pistols, his deadly aim claiming two lives before he was overpowered. Even then, he managed to bury his knife to the hilt; as razor-sharp bayonets and two bullets to the head claimed his own life.

On the chapel roof, Almeron Dickinson and his crew showered nails and scrap iron from their 12-pounders, ripping the Mexicans in the plaza.

At that moment, Morales and the remainder of his troops lugged the 18-pounder around and raked the chapel's stout bulwark. Strong oak doors blew open. Platforms fell. Dickinson went down. So did Jim Bonham. As the scaffolding crashed to the dirt, six others perished.

With the heavy doors swaying on broken hinges the Mexicans rushed through. Gregorio Esparza fell to a lead ball in the chest and a bayonet to the side.

Gunner Robert Evans, badly wounded, crawled with a torch to the powder room.

"Should the Alamo be overrun, blow everything to smithereens," had been Travis' order on March 5th.

He never made it.

Bunched in the rear of the chapel were the women and children, too frightened to move. Only one young boy dared to rise as the troops approached. He was shot as he drew a blanket around his shivering shoulders.

Next, two boys aged eleven and twelve — the sons of gunner Anthony Wolf —were bayoneted beside their father.

Enrique Esparza recoiled against a cold wall, certain his young life was about to end. Surprisingly, he was spared. Possibly one or more of the soldiers recognized him.

Brigado Guerrero, a defender from Béxar, kneeled imploringly when a woman he was hiding behind was shoved aside. He was just a prisoner, he pleaded, taken by the Anglo-Americans against his will. He had been for Santa Anna all along. "Viva Santa Anna!" They believed him and let him go.

In the sacristy, Susanna Dickinson anxiously awaited her fate. There were other women in the room, but she seemed not to notice. Her only concern was for little Angelina Elizabeth, clinging desperately to her apron.

She heard heavy footfalls, shouts and curses outside the door. Then, with an abrupt crash, it flew open and gunner Jacob Walker of her husband's crew burst in, followed by four Mexican soldiers.

Susanna fell to her knees in prayer, holding tighter to Angelina. Walker scampered from wall to corner, trying to hide. He was shot, then hoisted aloft like stuck fodder and carried triumphantly out to the plaza.

By 6:30 a.m. everything grew silent. Only the slow, incessant dripping of blood made any sound.

The Alamo had fallen.

Beneath the north wall laid the body of Colonel William Barret Travis.

Between the Long Barrack and the southeast palisade, David Crockett still held a death-grip on a Mexican soldier. His "Tennessee boys" lay sprawled on either side.

The Long Barrack presented a mass of Texian corpses.

On the southwest wall, Captain William Carey and his artillerymen lay stilled forever.

In the Low Barracks, Jim Bowie's mutilated remains stretched on its cot. Beside it lay three blue and white uniforms, one with the handle of a large knife protruding from its middle.

Of the dead in the chapel: 11 were defenders, 3 noncombatants.

The Mexican army joyously awaited arrival of His Excellency, General López de Santa Anna, to inspect the work of their courage.

Around 6:35 a.m., Susanna Dickinson, Señora Gregorio Esparza and her children, and other survivors were taken to a little room near the main entrance to the chapel.

It had not yet been decided what to do with them.

At 6:45 a.m., a Mexican officer appeared in the entrance.

"Is there a Mrs. Dickinson here?"asked the officer quietly.

Susanna hesitated.

"If you value your life, speak up!" Almonte snapped.

Carrying Angelina, she stepped forward.

"Come, the General has need of you."

Following Almonte outside, she winced at the glittering light. How long had it been since she had seen the sun?

In the yard the Mexicans were drinking, celebrating their glorious victory.

One drunken soldier aimed his musket and fired, hitting Susanna in the calf. She slumped to the ground, Angelina slipping from her grasp.

"Let her alone!" shouted Almonte in Spanish, ordering two of his staggering men to each carry the young woman and her frightened daughter.

In shock, fear and pain, Susanna would remember very little of what happened next. She did, however, recall one grisly scene:

> **"Colonel Crockett lying dead and mutilated between the church and the two-story** [long] **barrack; I even remember seeing his peculiar cap by his side."**

Soon, others were escorted to the plaza.

From the chapel, Anna Salazar Esparza, her four children, María de Jesús, Enrique, Manuel, Francisco; their elder relative, Petra Gonzales; Bettie, Negro garrison cook; Concepción Losoya, mother of defender José Toribio Losoya, and his younger brother, Juan; Juana Melton, Mexican wife of defender Eliel Melton; Victoriana de Salina and her three children; and Concepción Losoya, wife of José Toribio Losoya, with her boy and two girls.

Juana Alsbury with her baby and sister Gertrudis, whom Bowie had sheltered in the west wall for safety, walked out among the rubble.

Oblivious to their surroundings, the group trudged to the south gate, where they were driven into town. Juana, her baby, and Gertrudis where taken to the Veramendi house, the rest to the home of Ramón Músquiz.

Back at the Alamo, the still celebrating Mexican army began shooting dead Texian bodies. They even destroyed a stray cat simply because, as one soldado would later boast: "It was Americano."

Walking through the compound, Santa Anna ordered all shooting stopped. He wished to inspect the bodies, as they lay, undisturbed.

Summoning for Joe, who had cautiously come from hiding, he asked him to identify the bodies of his master and Bowie. Though wounded himself, he did as he was asked.

Leading Béxar citizens were called in to "point out the bodies of several distinguished Texians."

One eyewitness, a 16-year-old fifer in the Mexican army

named Apolinario "Polin" Saldigua, later wrote of the survey:

> **"The bodies of the Texians lay as they had fallen; & many of them were covered by those Mexicans who had fallen upon them. The close of the struggle seemed to have been a hand-to-hand engagement, the number of slain Mexicans exceeding that of the Texians..."**

David Crockett's body must have been turned face up as the inspection party approached, for Saldigua's recounting continued:

> **"...**[Santa Anna] **wished to be conducted to the body of Cocket** [Crockett]**. This man lay with his face upward; & those of many Mexicans who had fallen upon him covered his body. His face was florid, like that of a living man; &, except for an ugly cut above his right eye & several bloody wounds, looked like a healthy man asleep. Santa Anna viewed him for a few moments, thrust his sword through him & turned away."**

Around this time, Santa Anna received news that a number of defenders had been captured.

A Mexican officer, writing anonymously for fear of reprisal, described the event:

> **"There were five** [defenders] **who hid themselves and when the action was over, General Castrillón found them and brought them into Santa Anna's presence who, for a**

moment reprimanded the said general, then turning his back, at which act, the soldiers already formed in a line, charged the prisoners and killed them."[28]

With the last rebels dead, Santa Anna called Secretary Caro to his side. He would dictate a victorious letter to General José María Tornel, Secretary of War and Navy, in Mexico City:

Most Excellent Sir:

Victory belongs to the army, which at this very moment, 8 o'clock a.m., achieved complete and glorious triumph that will render its memory imperishable.

The force at my disposal, recruits included, numbered 1400 infantry. This force, divided into four columns, and a reserve, commenced the attack at 5 o'clock a.m. They met with a stubborn resistance, the combat lasting more than an hour and a half, and the reserve having to be brought into action.

The fortress is now in our power, with its artillery, stores, etc. More than 600 corpses of foreigners were buried in the ditches and entrenchments, and a great many, who had escaped the bayonet of the infantry, fell in the vicinity under the sabres of the cavalry.

Among the corpses are those of Bowie and Travis, who styled themselves Colonels, and also that of Crockett, and several leading men... We lost about 70 men killed and 300 wounded, among them are 25 officers.

The bearer takes with him one of the enemy's battalions [flags], **captured today. The inspection of it will show plainly the true abettors, who came from the ports of the United States of the North.**

God and Liberty!

[signed] **Antonio López de Santa Anna**

Headquarters, Béxar, March 6, 1836

Secretary Caro, clearing his throat, read back the letter.

Nice touch, thought Santa Anna, sending the enemy flag home as proof that he had crushed the perfidious foreigners. With such a victory, no one would question his supremacy. It wasn't like thumping a gang of uprising peons. He had actually beaten the American eagle itself.

When Secretary Caro cleared his throat, there was a reason. Except for the captured flag and the length of the battle, Santa Anna's entire report comprised nothing but lies.

Of his total force, which numbered 2,400, he lost 600 killed by Texian fire, with 400 wounded, nearly one-half of his army. Of those who died from friendly fire, we can only guess.

Fortunately, Francisco Ruiz, Alcade of Béxar, left us this bit of information:

"Santa Anna directed me to call on some

> **of the neighbors to come with carts to carry the** [Mexican] **dead to the cemetery** [Campo Santo], **but not having sufficient room for them, I ordered some to be thrown into the river, which was done on the same day."**

The Texian dead ran far short of the 600 tallied by Santa Anna.

Now to dispose of the rebel corpses in a belittling, yet memorable fashion.

Santa Anna envisioned a huge fire towering high above the broken Alamo walls; it's blackened smoke seen for sundry miles.

Perfect!

"Burn them!" he told Almonte [29].

"Burn them!" he instructed Ruiz.

In a transcript, Ruiz recorded his sad task:

> **"Santa Anna sent a company of dragoons with me to bring wood and dry branches from the neighboring forests. At about 3 o'clock in the afternoon of March 6, we laid the wood and dry branches upon which a pile of dead bodies was placed, more wood was piled on them, then another pile of bodies were brought, and in this manner they were arranged in layers."**

To which Saldigua added:

> **"... Four soldiers walked around it; each**

carrying a can of camphine from which he squirted the liquid onto the pile."

At 5 p.m. three pyres were torched, two small pyres outskirting the Alamo walls, with the largest blazing inside the compound.

That was the end.

As Santa Anna had foreseen, disparaged smoke wafted high into the lavender sky.

Satisfied, he turned his horse and motioned for Almonte:

"Bring the Dickinson woman to my headquarters tomorrow morning."

"Come in, Mrs. Dickinson."

Santa Anna rose from behind his desk as Susanna, carrying Angelina, entered the Yturri house headquarters.

"I trust you have been treated well?"

Susanna limped to the desk, her calf heavily bandaged. Almonte had offered to hold the baby, but she refused to let him touch her.

Santa Anna helped Susanna to a chair and ordered Ben to bring her some coffee.

Ben, who was in fact Almonte's servant, nervously fumbled with a cup. His Excellency once threatened to "run him through" if his orders were not "obeyed instantly."

Santa Anna looked at Susanna's calf and shook his head.

"A terrible affair. If I find the wretch who did this, he will be shot."

All of a sudden, Susanna exploded into tears.

"Hasn't there been enough killing?"she shrieked. "What kind of a man are you? My husband! All the brave men!"

"Ah! But such are the fortunes of war, my dear."

Santa Anna reached for Angelina. Susanna pulled away, the child gripping her mother's neck.

Sighing, a bit frustrated, he returned to his desk.

"Such a beautiful child," he sat down. "It's a shame that she is an orphan. And with you a widow."

"Thanks to you!" It was hard to be cordial to her husband's murderer.

Santa Anna ignored the outburst.

"And, with you a widow," he continued, laboriously searching for words in English he found easy in Spanish, "you will need support. Your child, she will need the best education. I can give them to you. I have the most beautiful hacienda…"

"In Mexico?"

"Si," smiled Santa Anna. In Vera Cruz."

"No!"

"What!" No one had ever said no to His Excellency before.

"Your Excellency," broke in Almonte, who was casually sipping coffee near Ben. "Perhaps it would be best to send Mrs. Dickinson on the errand…"

"You are right, Colonel," Santa Anna answered in his native language. "This woman would be of no use to me at home. My wife, ugly though she is, submits to my every wish."

Almonte suppressed a chuckle.

Picking up a piece of paper, Santa Anna returned to English; all courteousness gone.

"Mrs. Dickinson, I have a message that you are to deliver to the people of Gonzales. It is written in English."

Handing her the paper, he stood above her.

"Resistance is hopeless, Mrs. Dickinson! Make them understand that!"

Stepping to the window facing the ruined Alamo, he excitedly waved his right hand towards the glass.

"This will be the treatment of all those who oppose me! Do you understand?"

She understood.

"Good! I will give you a horse. Ben will escort you. He is of no further use to me."

Colonel Almonte started to object. Then, observing his leader's stern expression discreetly finished his coffee.

On Friday, March 11th, a grief-stricken Susanna Dickinson, cradling her baby, rode silently past the deserted Alamo. Beside her trotted Ben, guiding her horse to Gonzales.

A strong wind blew from the north. A wailing that made the little party cringe deep into their mounts.

Unfortunately for Santa Anna, his message had a decisively reverse effect on the peoples of the world. News of the massacre swept across Texas, across America, across the oceans. Shouts that no one should ever forget the Alamo reverberated throughout all corners of the globe.

In New York, the ***Post*** headlined their reaction:

TYRANT! BUTCHER!

Santa Anna will shortly see that policy would have required that he govern himself by the rules of civilized warfare.

Had he treated the vanquished with moderation and generosity, it would have been difficult, if not impossible, to awaken the general sympathy for the people of Texas, which now impels so many adventurous and ardent spirits to throng to the aid of their brethren.

The *Memphis Enquirer* wrote:

We have been opposed to the Texas war from first to last, but our feelings we cannot suppress — some of our own bosom friends have fallen in the Alamo. We would avenge their deaths and spill the last drop of our blood upon the alter of Liberty.

Most especially mourned was David Crockett.

From Tennessee to Washington City, they lamented his death.

His wife Elizabeth bought a black dress. She would wear it in public until her own passing on January 31, 1860, in Hood County, Texas [30].

His children, grown and small, awaited his return; sure it was all a mistake. But, when months passed without the familiar "Hullo th' house, I'm home," they knew their "paw" would never come back.

Even President Jackson bowed his shaggy head when he read the report. "I cannot fully express," he said in a private conversation, "how much this man's [Crockett's] death has affected me. His violent passing saddens me deeply."

Still negotiating purchase of Texas from Mexico, Jackson would not publicly denounce the nation; nor would he reprove its commander-in-chief.

Yet, the average citizen was not of the same mind. If taking no sides on the Texas issue, they adored the warm, companionable and gentle David "Davy" Crockett. How could anyone kill him?

The ***Natchez Courier*** soon voiced its outrage, syndicating it across America and Europe from the smallest hamlet to the largest city:

> **Poor Davy Crockett! We lament the fate of the sick Bowie. We feel sad and angry, by turns, when we think of the butchery of the gallant Travis. But there is something in the untimely end of the poor Tennessean that almost wrings a tear from us. It is too bad — by all that is good — it is too bad. The quaint, the laughter-moving, but the fearless upright Crockett, to be butchered by such a wretch as Santa Anna, is not to be borne.**

On April 21, 1836, eight hundred enraged volunteers, led by General Sam Houston, victoriously routed Santa Anna's 1,250 troops at San Jacinto.

The battle — or more accurately the slaughter — lasted

18 minutes. Santa Anna was captured, trembling and disguised as a "common foot soldier," fleeing the bloodbath.

Brought before Houston the following day, Santa Anna asked for his medicine bottle. Surrounding him, armed to the teeth and awaiting orders to shoot, stood the newly named **Texans**.

Houston, his ankle shattered by an enemy musket ball during the engagement, lay propped against an oak tree.

"General Santa Anna! Ah! Indeed!" he exclaimed with a smile, employing Colonel Almonte's translating skills.

"Take a seat, General. I'm glad to see you."

He motioned to an ammunition box.

"Take a seat. Your medicine will be here shortly."

Sure he was about to suffer the fate of his past victims he shakily sat down.

His conqueror was too kind, too warm. Such ceremony usually presaged executions of high-ranking officials. He didn't want to die. He wanted to live.

"I am General Antonio López de Santa Anna, President of Mexico, Commander-in-Chief of the Army of Operations," he spoke nervously, his hands quivering, "and I put myself at the disposition of the brave General Houston. I wish to be treated as a general should when a prisoner of war."

"We'll talk about that later, General. Ah! Here's your Medicine!"

Eagerly grabbing for the bottle, Santa Anna pried it open and took an unusually large dosage.

"Feeling better, General?"

Assuaged by effects of the opium, Santa Anna ostentatiously addressed his captor:

"That a man may consider himself born to no common destiny who has conquered the Napoléon of the West, it now remains for him to be generous to the vanquished."

"You should have thought of that at the Alamo and Goliard!" frowned Houston.

"He is gone from among us, and is no more to be seen in the walks of men, but in his death like Sampson, slew more of his enemies than in all his life. Even his most bitter enemies here, I believe, have buried all animosity, and join the general lamentation over his untimely end."

John Wesley Crockett
(1807-1852)
From a eulogistic speech on his father.
(November 28, 1837)

Epilogue

Santa Anna's life would not end for another forty years. Enfeebled by a wooden right leg, nearly blind from cataracts and in poverty, he fell into a deep sleep during a warm night in June of 1876, at the age of 82.

Sam Houston, defending his position in not exacting revenge on Mexico's despotic ruler, later wrote:

> **My motive in sparing the life of Santa Anna was to relieve the country of all hostile enemies without further bloodshed, and secure his acknowledgment of our independence, in which I considered of vastly more importance than the mere gratification of revenge.**

His scenario proved correct. Santa Anna still had over 4,000 effective troops in Texas, with some 2,500 under the command of General Vicente Filísola less than 50 miles away. His army, fatigued from long marches and the battle, would stand little chance against a Mexican force consisting of this magnitude. An execution would not free Texas. Negotiation would.

Within two days, Santa Anna's entire Mexican cogency packed up and left Texas on receiving a dispatch ending with:

> **...I have agreed with General Houston upon an armistice, which may put an end to the war forever.**
> [signed] **Antonio López de Santa Anna**

Santa Anna remained in captivity until February of 1837.

On May 14, 1836, he had signed the Treaties of Velasco, recognizing Texas' independence — with the Rio Grande bordering her to the south — knowing full well his Congress would repudiate any agreement made by a prisoner under duress.

Nevertheless, Texas immediately acted upon the treaties.

Electing Houston its president on September 5, 1836, the new republic sent an emissary to Washington City with a request for recognition or annexation. President Jackson, however, fearing political repercussions, sat on the requisition until March 2, 1837, his last day in office, before signing for recognition of the Lone Star Republic's independence.

Jackson's successor, Martin Van Buren, sidestepped annexation altogether. Van Buren's successor, William Henry Harrison, had little time to do anything at all, succumbing to viral pneumonia one month after taking office.

Harrison's successor, John Tyler, pressed for annexation, yet was unable to instruct Andrew Jackson Donelson, former-president Jackson's nephew and his Texas representative, to announce the measure until March 3, 1845, one day prior to leaving office.

On December 29, 1845, President James Knox Polk officially welcomed Texas into the Union.

On Thursday, February 19, 1846, almost ten years subsequent to the Alamo's fall, Texas raised a galaxy of twenty-eight stars, embraced in thirteen red and white stripes, beside her beloved Lone Star.

Texas had won her hard-bitten fight for independence.

Meanwhile, Santa Anna had returned to power in Mexico.

With a far-reaching goal — to retake Texas and prevent the United States from acquiring California — he would survive defeats, humiliations and charges of corruption; all leading to his final and eternal disgrace.

Sam Houston represented the state of Texas for thirteen years in the U.S. Senate, returning home as her 7th governor in 1859.

Although deposed from office in 1861 for opposing her secessionist movements, he refused to leave his state when she officially joined the Confederacy on March 16, 1861.

"I have seen Texas pass through one long, bloody war," he sadly confided to a friend on March 18th, the day he vacated his seat. "I do not wish to involve her in civil strife. I have done all I could to keep her from seceding and now if she won't go with me I will have to turn and go with her."

Retiring in seclusion to his home in Huntsville, he would not live to see the devastation caused his beloved Texas by the Civil War. On July 26, 1863, at 6:16 p.m., he closed his eyes murmuring to his wife "Texas, Texas, Margaret" repeatedly, until his lips ceased to move.

On March 9, 1836, the last burning ember fell to ash. The funeral pyres smoldered and slightly crackled. Of once proud men, only charred fragments of flesh clinging to blackened bones and teeth remained.

For nearly a year the remains laid exposed to ravenous animals and an angry land. Then, on February 25, 1837, the recently promoted Colonel Juan Sequin, by order of the Lone Star Republic's President Houston, collected whatever traces were left and solemnly placed everything into a large coffin. Engraved on the coffin lid were the names of Travis, Bowie and Crockett, in representation of "all those who laid down their lives."

Draped in the Lone Star flag, it was buried with full military honor in a peach orchard 300 yards from the fort.

The orchard no longer exists. The exact interment location remains unknown [1].

Through shattered windows and doors a frenzied wind blew, as if the Alamo echoed a somber refrain.

Once more, the mission San Antonio de Valero yielded to the elements.

"When I first saw the Alamo in 1845," wrote one elderly Texan, remembering his boyhood, "it was a veritable ruin, partly from the destruction caused by the battle, but mostly from its abandonment as the adobe of men.

"No doors or windows shut out the sunshine or storm; millions of bats inhabited the crevices in the walls and flat dirt roofs, and in the twilight the bats would pour forth in myriad.

"It was a meeting place for owls; weeds and grass grew from the walls and flat dirt roofs, and even the cacti plant decorated the tumble-down roof of the old building [Long Barrack] that flanked the church.

"In the south wall of the chapel was a breach near the ground, said to have been made by Santa Anna's cannon [2].

"We boys could run up the embankment of the chapel to the outer wall and onto the roof of the convent building. [To us] it was a famous playground."

"Those who would give up essential Liberty, to purchase a little temporary Safety, deserves neither Liberty nor Safety"

Benjamin Franklin
(1706–1790)

David Stern Crockett
(1786–1836)

David "Davy" Crockett, as he appeared in this congressial painting. He complained that portraits like this made him "look like a cross betwixt a clean-cut member o' Congress an' a' Methodist preacher." (Image courtesy: Library of Congress.)

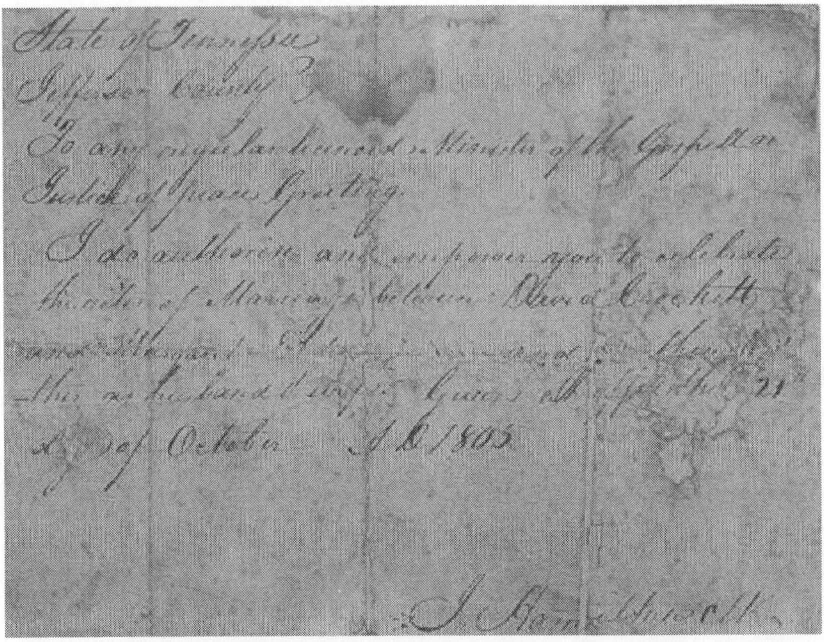
State of Tennessee
Jefferson County
To any regular licensed Minister of the Gospel or
Justice of Peace Greeting
I do authorize and empower you to celebrate
the rites of Marriage between David Crockett
and Margaret Elder [illegible]
[illegible] as husband & wife [illegible] this 21st
day of October A D 1805
[illegible]

Never used contract for David Crockett's proposed marriage to Margaret Elder, dated October 21, 1805. (Preserved by: Jefferson County Courthouse, Dandridge, Tennessee.)

Massacre at Fort Mims, August 30, 1813

Initiating the Creek War, this onslaught would ultimately undo William Weatherford [Red Eagle] **and his Red Sticks.** (Image courtesy: Fort Mims Restoration Association, Baldwin County, Alabama.)

Battle of Horseshoe Bend, March 27, 1814

This engagement literally crushed the hostile Creeks' [Red Sticks'] **will and capacity to wage further war.** (Image courtesy: Culver Pictures, Inc., 51-02 21st St., Long Island, New York.)

General Andrew Jackson encounters William Weatherford [Chief Red Eagle] **at Fort Jackson, Alabama after the Battle of Horseshoe Bend.** (Image courtesy: Library of Congress.)

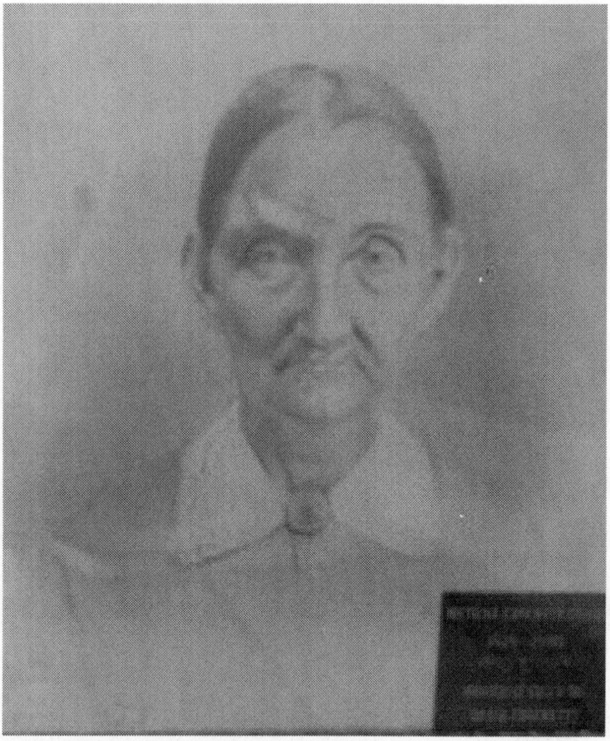

Matilda Crockett Fields, age 68
(1821–1890)

The youngest and last surviving daughter of David and Elizabeth Patton Crockett (Photo courtesy: Crockett Cabin/Museum, 219 N. Trenton St., Old Highway 45 West, Rutherford, Tennessee.)

001_002_2.28
Painting by Robert Lindneux. Woolaroc Museum, Bartlesville, Oklahoma.

Trail of Tears of 1838

Though history traditionally observes the Cherokee migration to the Indian Territory as a singular Trail of Tears, all Native Americans to this day may justifiably dispute this viewing. (From 1942 painting by Robert Lindneux (1871–1970), Woolaroc Museum, Bartlesville, Oklahoma. Courtesy: Facts on File, Inc., 132 West. 31st St., 17th Floor, New York, N.Y.)

Adam "Timbertoes" Huntsman
(1786–1849)

If not for this bombastic lawyer and politician defeating David Crockett in his bid for congressional reelection in 1835, he would have missed the Battle of the Alamo and his final legendary status. (Image courtesy: Library of Congress.)

General Martín Perfecto de Cos
(1800–1854)

Santa Anna's inept brother-in-law was sent to arrest the Texian rebels in 1835, only to surrender and return to Mexico in disgrace. (Image from: John Frost's ***Pictorial History of Mexico and the Mexican War***. Publishers: Harold & Murray, Richmond, Virginia, 1848.)

The Cos House

Predating 1835, this building was the site of General Martín de Cos' signing of the Articles of Capitulation following his defeat by the Texian army on December 9, 1835. (Photo courtesy: La Villita Historic Arts Village, 418 Villita #903, San Antonio, Texas,)

Edward Burleson
(1798–1851)

Following surrender of Mexican General Cos in December of 1835, the then Major General Burleson rode smugly out of the Alamo, convinced the war with Mexico had reached its satisfactory conclusion. (Photo courtesy: Texas State Library and Archives Commission, 1201 Brazos, Austin, Texas.)

A rare portrait of
James "Jim" Bowie
(1796–1836)
(Image courtesy: Texas State Library and Archives Comission)

Lt. Colonel William Barret Travis
(1809–1836)

This is an idealized portrait of the Alamo commander, complete with a fanciful uniform. Unfortunately, none of Travis' pictorial likenesses can be considered reliable. (Image courtesy: Texas State Library and Archives Commission.)

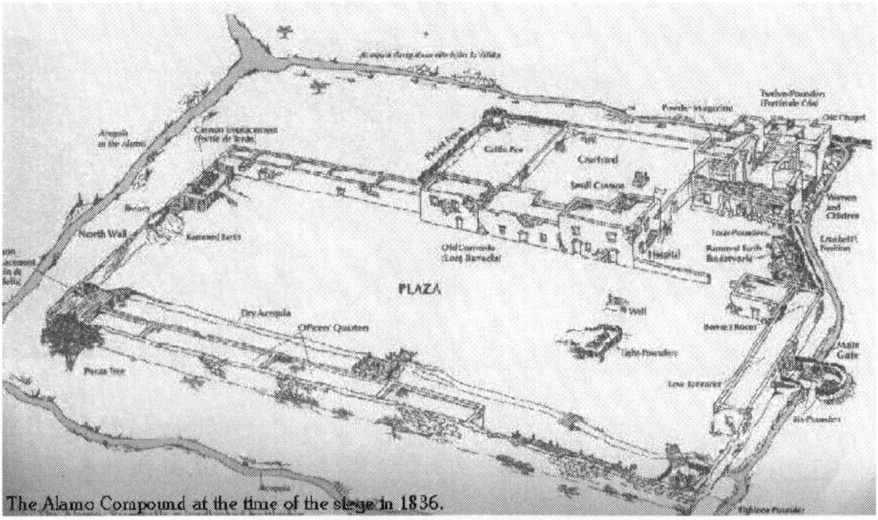

The Alamo Compound at the time of the siege in 1836.

The Alamo in 1836

The siege of the Alamo began on February 23, 1836; the actual battle lasting 12 days. The final assault took place in the early hours of March 6th, with General Antonio López de Santa Anna commanding his army from the new battery [also referred to as the "north battery"] **north of the fortress. Lt. Colonel William Barret Travis commanded the Texian defenders from his post on the north wall. At the sound of "*Deguello* — the song of death!" four Mexican columns struck the fort simultaneously. The final onslaught lasted ninety minutes, with all remaining defenders dying for a cause in which they believed.** (Image courtesy: The Center for American History, Map Collection, The University of Texas at Austin.)

General Antonio López de Santa Anna
(1794–1876)

Although ruthless and sly, under his strongman dictatorship Mexico lost a third of its acquired territory, (Image courtesy: Texas State Library and Archives Commission.)

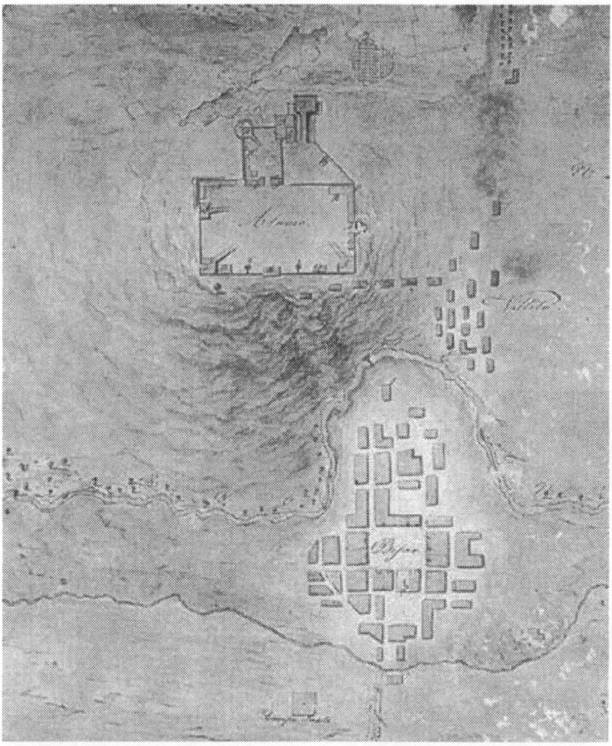

Santa Anna's Battle Plan of the Alamo Siege

Drawn by Colonel Ygnacio de Labastida, Commander of Engineers for the Mexican army in 1836, this technically correct map shows Béxar situated 400 yards across the San Antonio River to the west. To the south of the Alamo stood the outlying houses of La Villita, destroyed by the defenders to deny protection for the attacking Mexican forces early in the battle. (Map image courtesy: Barker Texas History Center, The University of Texas at Austin.)

Colonel Juan Nepomuceno Seguín
(1806–1890)

During the Alamo siege Seguín and his aide, Antonio Cruz, rode through the Mexican lines to deliver Travis' dispatch to Sam Houston.

In 1837, he would return to give full military honor to the Alamo defenders. (Image courtesy: Texas State Library and Archives Commission.)

General José de Urrea
(1797–1849)

He defeated Colonel Frank Johnson and his small detachment of Texians in the Battle of San Patricio at 3a.m on the morning of February 27, 1836.

Although a victorious Mexican leader throughout the Texas Campaign, he was bitterly opposed to Santa Anna's decisions to slaughter prisoners. (Photo courtesy: Texas State Library and Archives Commission.)

General Pedro de Ampudia
(1803–1868)

Served as Santa Anna's lieutenant colonel and general artillery commander during the Alamo siege. (Photo courtesy: Texas State Library and Archives Commission.)

James Butler Bonham
(1807–1836)

An unlikely-appearing hero, Jim Bonham is best remembered for having returned to the Alamo with a despondent message for Colonel Travis, breaking through enemy lines to immortal valor. (Photo courtesy: Texas State Library and Archives Commission.)

Colonel James Walker Fannin, Jr.
(1805–1836)

Following his refusal to James Butler Bonham's plea for aid, he made a half-hearted attempt to relieve the Alamo. (Image courtesy: Texas State Library and Archives Commission.)

Benjamin Franklin "Uncle Ben" Highsmith (1817–1905)

One of the first messengers to leave Béxar with an appeal from Travis to Colonel Fannin, then 19-year-old Ben Highsmith tried unsuccessfully to persuade Jim Bonham not to return to the doomed fort.

He would later join the Texas Rangers under Captain John Hays of the Somervell Expedition in 1842. (Photo from A. J. Sowell's ***Early Settlers and Indian Fighters of Southwest Texas***. Publishers: Ben C. Jones, Printers, 1900.)

Pictured is the gold cat's-eye ring strung about the neck of 15-month-old Angelina Dickinson by Colonel Travis on March 5, 1836. (Now in the Alamo museum,) (Photo courtesy: Texas State Library and Archives commission.)

General Juan Nepomuceno Almonte
(1803–1869)

As Santa Anna wrote Mexico City of his glorious victory over the Alamo rebels, the then Colonel Almonte privately noted: "One more such glorious victory and we are finished." (Photo courtesy: Texas State Library and Archives Commission.)

General Sam Houston
(1793–1863)

Although not believing in the Alamo's strife until it was too late, he would victoriously lead his volunteers in the Battle of San Jacinto on April 21, 1836. (Image courtesy: University of Texas at Austin.)

General Sidney Sherman
(1805–1873)

Born in Marlboro, Massachusetts, Sherman led the Second Regiment of the Texas Volunteers as a lieutenant colonel during the Battle of San Jacinto, and is credited with coining the famous battle cry: "Remember the Alamo! Remember Goliard!" (Image courtesy: Texas State Library and Archives Commission.)

San Jacinto

General Antonio López de Santa Anna is brought before the wounded Sam Houston on April 22, 1836, following his flight and capture at the Battle of San Jacinto. "Deaf" Smith, Houston's able scout, is to the right in the painting. (Painting image courtesy: San Jacinto Museum of History, 1 Monument Circle, La Porte, Texas)

General Vicente Filísola
(1789–1850)

Filísola was Santa Anna's unfortunate scapegoat for his defeat at San Jacinto. In his reports and memoirs, he claimed to have given Filísola orders to join him [at San Jacinto] **by forced march to reinforce an attack on Houston's army.**

Filísola, as a matter of fact, received no word from Santa Anna until his dispatch to withdraw all remaining forces to Mexico following his capitulation. (Image courtesy: San Jacinto Museum of History.)

Andrew Jackson
(1767–1845)
7th President of the United States
(1829–1837)

Ever the conniving politician, Jackson would not sign for Texas' recognition until his last day in office. (Image courtesy: Library of Congress.)

John Tyler
(1790–1862)
10th President of the United States
(1841–1845)

Tyler favored annexation of Texas from the inception of his presidency, yet was delayed in announcing his decision prior to one day of leaving office. (Image courtesy: Library of Congress.)

James Knox Polk
(1795–1849)
11th President of the United States
(1845–1849)

President Polk officially welcomed Texas into the Union as the 28th state on December 29, 1845. (Photo: Mathew Brady's studio, 1849. Courtesy: Library of Congress.)

Andrew Jackson, age 78

He would argue the correctness of his precautionary decision on the Texas recognition issue for the remainder of his days. (A daguerreotype of Andrew Jackson shortly before his death in 1845, believed taken by the early business associate of famous Civil War photographer Mathew Brady, Edward Anthony (1819–1888). Courtesy: Libray of Congress.)

Antonio López de Santa Anna in 1847

This photograph was taken shortly after he directed his country in the Battle of Buena Vista, in which both sides claimed victory, during the Mexican-American War (1846–1848). (Photo courtesy: Texas State Library and Archives Commission.)

Sam Houston, age 70
7th Governor of Tennessee (1827–1829)
1st President of the Republic of Texas (1836–1838)
3rd President of the Republic of Texas (1841–1844)
United States Senator (1846–1859)
7th Governor of Texas (1859–1861)

Sam Houston died of pneumonia on July 26, 1863 at his rented home, Steamboat House, in Huntsville, Texas.

Holding his wife's hand as he passed on, he whispered repeatedly "Texas, Texas, Margaret." (Daguerreotype by Mathew Brady. Courtesy: Library of Congress.)

"Texas has yet to learn submission, come from what source it may."

Sam Houston
(1793–1863)

Appendix A

Who Died at the Alamo?

One of the mysteries surrounding the Alamo is the number of men who died defending her on March 6, 1836.

Through the years figures ranging from 181 to as high as 254 have perplexed both chronicler and reader alike.

Reasons for the confusion comprise these:

- Travis sent out couriers who never returned.
- Many Tejano defenders slipped out before the final assault.
- A small contingent entered the Alamo during a lull in the fighting on March 5th.
- Louis Rose deserted
- "Brigado" Guerrero talked his way to preservation.

So what is the final count?

The following updated roster places a count of 193 [1].

ROSTER OF DEFENDERS WHO DIED AT THE ALAMO — WITH THEIR LAST KNOWN ADDRESS:

1. Albamilo, Juan — San Antonio
2. Allen, R.
3. Ambrose, Miles DeForest — Texas
4. Autry, Micajah — Tennessee
5. Badillo, Juan A. — San Antonio
6. Baily, Peter James — Kentucky
7. Baker, Isaac — Gonzales, Texas
8. Baker, William Charles M. — Missouri
9. Ballentine, John J. — Texas
10. Ballentine, Robert W. — Scotland
11. Baugh John J. — Virginia
12. Baxter, Joseph
13. Bayless, Joseph — Tennessee
14. Blair, John — Tennessee
15. Blair, Samuel B. — Tennessee
16. Blazeby, William — England
17. Bonham, James Butler — Texas
18. Bourne, Daniel — England
19. Bowie, James — Texas
20. Bowman, Jessie B. — Texas
21. Brown, George — England
22. Brown, James — Pennsylvania

23. Brown, Robert
24. Buchanan, James — Alabama
25. Burns, Samuel E. — Ireland
26. Butler, George D. — Missouri
27. Campbell, Robert — Tennessee
28. Cane (Cain), John — Pennsylvania
29. Carey, William R. — Virginia
30. Clark, Charles Henry — Missouri
31. Clark, M.B. — Nacogdoches, Texas
32. Cloud, Daniel William — Kentucky
33. Cochran, Robert E. — New Jersey
34. Cottle, George Washington — Tennessee
35. Courtman, Henry — Germany
36. Crawford, Lemuel — South Carolina
37. Crockett, David — Tennessee
38. Crossman, Robert — Massachusetts
39. Cummings, David P. — Pennsylvania
40. Cunningham, Robert — New York
41. Darst, Jacob C. — Kentucky
42. Davis, John — Kentucky
43. Day, Freeman H.K. — Gonzales, Texas
44. Day, Jerry C. — Missouri
45. Daymon, Squire — Tennessee
46. Dearduff, William — Tennessee
47. Dennison, Stephen — England
48. Despallier, Charles — Louisiana
49. Dickinson, Almeron — Gonzales, Texas
50. Dillard, John H. — Tennessee
51. Dimpkins, James R. — England
52. Duel, Lewis — New York

53. Duvalt, Andrew — Ireland
54. Edwards, Samuel
55. Edwards, William
56. Espallier, Carlos — San Antonio
57. Esparza, Gregorio (José María) — San Antonio
58. Evans, Robert — Ireland
59. Evans, Samuel B. — New York
60. Ewing, James L. — Tennessee
61. Fishbaugh, William — Gonzales, Texas
62. Flanders, John — Massachusetts
63. Floyd, Dolphin Ward — North Carolina
64. Forsyth, John Hubbard — New York
65. Fluentes, Antonio — San Antonio
66. Fuqua, Galba — Gonzales, Texas
67. Furtleroy, William H. — Kentucky
68. Garnett, William — Tennessee
69. Garrand, James W. — Louisiana
70. Garrett, James Girard — Tennessee
71. Garvin, John E. — Gonzales, Texas
72. Gaston, John E. — Kentucky
73. George, James — Gonzales, Texas
74. Goodrich, James Camp — Tennessee
75. Gordon, Pelitiah
76. Grimes, Albert Calvin — Georgia
77. Gwynne, James C. — England
78. Hannan, James — Texas
79. Harris, John — Kentucky
80. Harrison, Andrew Jackson
81. Harrison, William B. — Ohio
82. Haskell (Heiskell), Charles M. — Tennessee

83.Hawkins, Joseph M. — Ireland
84.Hays, John M. — Tennessee
85.Herndon, Patrick Henry — Virginia
86.Hersee, William D. — England
87.Holland, Tapley — Ohio
88.Holloway, Samuel — Pennsylvania
89.Howell, William D. — Massachusetts
90.Jackson, William Daniel — Ireland
91.Jackson, Thomas — Ireland
92.Jameson, Green B. — Texas
93.Jennings, Gordon C. — Connecticut
94.Jimenéz, Damacio (Damasio)
95.Johnson, Lewis — Wales
96.Johnson, William — Pennsylvania
97.Jones, John — New York
98.Kellogg, John B. (Johnnie) — Gonzales, Texas
99.Kenney, James — Virginia
100.Kent, Andrew — Kentucky
101.Kerr, Joseph — Louisiana
102.Kimbell (Kimble), George C. — New York
103.King, William P. — Gonzales, Texas
104.Lewis, William Irvine — Virginia
105.Lightfoot, William J. — Virginia
106.Lindley, Jonathan L. — Illinois
107.Linn, William — Massachusetts
108.Losoya, (José) Toribio D. — San Antonio
109.Main, George Washington — Virginia
110.Malone, William T. — Georgia
111.Marshall, William — Tennessee
112.Martin, Albert — Gonzales, Texas

113.McCafferty, Edward — Texas
114.McClelland, Ross
115.McCoy, Jesse — Gonzales, Texas
116.McDowell, William — Pennsylvania
117.McGee, James — Ireland
118.McGregor, John — Scotland
119.McKinney, Robert — Ireland
120.Melton, Eliel — Georgia
121.Miller, Thomas R. — Tennessee
122.Mills, William — Tennessee
123.Millsaps, Isaac — Mississippi
124.Mitchasson, Edward F. — Virginia
125.Mitchell, Edwin T. — Georgia
126.Mitchell, Napoleon B.
127.Moore, Robert B. — Virginia
128.Moore, Willis — Mississippi
129.Musselman, Robert — Ohio
130.Nava, Andres — San Antonio
131.Neggan, George — South Carolina
132.Nelson, Andrew M. — Tennessee
133.Nelson, Edward — South Carolina
134.Nelson, George — South Carolina
135.Northcross, James — Virginia
136.Nowlan, James — Ireland
137.Pagan, George — Mississippi
138.Parker, Christopher — Mississippi
139.Parks, William — North Carolina
140.Richardson, Perry — Texas
141.Pollard, Amos — Massachusetts
142.Reynolds, John Perry — Pennsylvania

143.Roberts, Thomas H.
144.Robinson Isaac — Scotland
145.Robertson, James Waters — Tennessee/Louisiana
146.Rose, James M. — Ohio [2]
147.Rusk, Jackson J. — Ireland
148.Rutherford, Jackson J. — Kentucky
149.Ryan, Isaac — Louisiana
150.Scurlock, Mial — North Carolina
151.Sewell, Marcus L. — England
152.Shield, Manson — Georgia
153.Simmons, Cleveland Kinloch — South Carolina
154.Smith, Andrew H. — Tennessee
155.Smith, Charles S. — Maryland
156.Smith, Joshua G. — North Carolina
157.Smith, William H. — Nacogdoches, Texas
158.Starr, Richard — England
159.Stewart, James E. — England
160.Stockton, Richard L. — Virginia
161.Summerlin, A. Spain — Tennessee
162.Summers, William E. — Tennessee
163.Sutherland, William D. — Alabama
164.Taylor, Edward — Tennessee
165.Taylor, George — Tennessee
166.Taylor, James — Tennessee
167.Taylor, William — Tennessee
168.Thomas, B. Archer M. — Kentucky
169.Thomas, Henry — Germany
170.Thompson, Jesse G. — Arkansas
171.Thomson, John W. — North Carolina
172.Thurston, John M. — Pennsylvania

173. Trammel, Burke — Ireland
174. Travis, William Barret — Texas
175. Tumlinson, George W. — Missouri
176. Tylee, James — New York
177. Walker, Asa — Tennessee
178. Walker, Jacob — Nacogdoches, Texas
179. Ward, William B. — Ireland
180. Warnell, Henry — Arkansas
181. Washington, Joseph G. — Tennessee
182. Waters, Thomas — England
183. Wells, William — Georgia
184. White, Isaac — Kentucky
185. White, Robert — Gonzales, Texas
186. Williamson, Hiram J. — Pennsylvania
187. Wills, William — Brazoria County, Texas
188. Wilson, David L. — Nacogdoches, Texas
189. Wilson, John — Pennsylvania
190. Wolf, Anthony (Avram) — England
191. Wright, Claiborne — North Carolina
192. Zanco, Charles — Denmark
193. John, Black Freedman (called John Desauque [3])

Appendix B

Who Survived the Alamo Siege?

In all, there were seventeen known survivors of the siege. Of these, three were American.

Susanna Wlkerson Dickinson left the Alamo a heroine in the beginning; where her hometown of Gonzales gathered to anxiously hear of her ordeal, console her loss, cry with her, and pry her with questions on the number of troops Santa Anna had when he attacked Béxar.

The newly appointed General Sam Houston, readying Gonzales and Texas for a retreat tensely given as the "Runaway Scrape," asked her to recount every facet of her nightmarish experience in minutest detail. He hoped to use this information for retaliation when his forces mobilized.

But, with her information exhausted, she was cast aside. Tossed to a world her young, uneducated, mind failed to comprehend. Even General Houston aversely refused her when she asked Texas to support her and Angelina.

"Texas is too poor," he simply said.

Susanna wheeled from this blow as if she had returned to the pounding blackness of the hellishness she just left, holding Angelina to the protection of her apron.

With all she had been through her own country objected to giving her even a small pension to placate her anguish. A bittersweet truth awakened in her fogged brain.

For a time she tried to make an honest living, yet needed a male protector. In June of 1837, she would cohabitate with a John Williams, whom she married on November 27, 1837.

Williams beat her unmercifully, which eventually caused a life-threatening miscarriage. She then took Angelina and filed for divorce, receiving it on March 24, 1838.

Next, she met a tranquil man named Francis P. Herring, offering her hand in marriage on December 20, 1838. This union occasioned nearly five happy years for the sad young woman. Unfortunately, Herring passed away on September 15, 1843, leaving the mother and daughter to wander alone once more.

On December 15, 1847, still hoping for male guidance, she married drayman Peter Bellis and opened a small boarding house, taking in laundry to make ends meet. Within ten years, however, Bellis filed a divorce petition, claiming she had "taken up residence in a house of ill fame."

Running with a fast crowd in 1837, Susanna had met and befriended Pamelia Mann [1], proprietress of Houston's premier brothel in the early days of the Republic known as the Mansion House. "Some uproarious scenes were enacted there," recalled a wizened old customer years later. "I also remember seeing the beautiful and playful Miss Susanna there."

The city named for the man who had once turned her out without a penny now paid her whatever she desired.

In 1849, 26-year-old Dr. Rufus C. Burleson returned to resume his pastorate for the First Baptist Church of Houston.

"I have come back to save the worst sinners in Houston," he announced, planting his eyes on a newly opened bordel.

He aimed a reproving finger at its opulent windows.

"Tomorrow afternoon, at the river. Be there!" he blared.

Susanna, with several associated courtesans laughingly accepted the challenge after a night of revelry, joining with an assemblage forming the banks of Buffalo Bayou.

Dr Burleson stood waist-deep in the shallow water near the embankment, and waved with a smile.

"Come, my flock, and be baptized into the light of the Lord. Come, my children. Come, and you will be sinless forevermore."

Slowly, cautiously, the gathering slogged toward the river.

The prostitutes remained still, clustered on a grassy knoll.

"See there, Reverend," crowed one of the harlots. "Only the righteous comes to you. The rest are back at our place enjoying a better type of baptism."

All the girls, except Susanna, giggled.

"I am here not to call the righteous, but sinners to repentance," answered Burleson, raising an animated hand above the assembly.

At that moment, something seemed to kindle Susanna's tortured brain. Long-dead images surfaced: The kind Colonel Crockett; the determined Colonel Travis; the outwardly fierce, yet gentle, Jim Bowie; and Almeron, the man she had truly loved.

Crockett was saying "Be sure you're right, Susanna."

Everyone gaped, especially the clumped cocottes, when Susanna moved down from the hill to the water.

"Among those who came forward with tears, and penitential sobs," wrote Burleson in his memoirs, "was Mrs. Dickinson, who had become Mrs. Bellis... After the baptism [her] change was so complete as to be observed by her neighbors, many who owed their life to her during the affliction [cholera epidemic]... I visited her in her home and wept and prayed with her. I found her a bundle of untamed passions, devoted to her love and bitter in her hate."

Although Susanna tried to change her ways over the next three years, she often strayed to her sinful life.

"Whenever she did wrong, especially in giving way to passion," continued Burleson, "she would confess and weep over it."

In the latter half of 1857, she married husband no. 5.

Joseph William Hannig was a German immigrant who fell in love, not with Susanna's looks, but with her "cabbage, bacon, and cornbread." Which was just as well, since she had gained so much weight over the past two years her alluring days were virtually ended.

In 1858, the couple packed up everything and moved to Austin, where they established a successful cabinet-making, furniture and undertaking business.

In 1862, she met the Rev. Dr. Burleson at a revival in Austin.

Grasping his hand, she said:

"Erring and wayward, but still struggling to do right and serve my redeemer."

She died in Austin, following an eight-month illness, on October 7, 1883. Tearfully, her husband inscribed her stone monument:

Sacred to the Memory of Susan A.
Wife of J.W. Hannig
Died Oct. 7, 1883
Aged 68
I Go to Prepare a Place for Thee

Hannig, sixteen years her junior, died in 1890. Although he later remarried, Joseph and Susanna lie together in Austin's Oakwood Cemetery. Closer than any other couple.

Angelic Angelina grew up anything but. Affectionately called "The Babe of the Alamo," she was a hell-raiser by the age of 15. At 16, she was married and bedding nearly every male friend of her husband, which led to a nettled break-up.

Following an inevitably bitter divorce, she turned her heart to prostitution. Not of financial necessity as had her mother — although Susanna later received the land grants she was seeking — but from "insatiable sexual desires."

Since Susanna was frequently called upon to testify before the State Legislature as to the legitimacy of land bounty claims made by relatives of the men who had perished at the Alamo, in 1850 she attempted to appropriate a public grant for Angelina's education, citing "... The child who had gone through the bloody siege and lost her father in it deserves to be educated by the state."

Guy Morrison Bryan [2], a nephew to Stephen F. Austin and member of the legislature, championed her plea. In a brilliant speech, handed down to us as ***The Defense of the Alamo Babe***, he said:

"I intended to remain silent on this occasion, but silence would now be a reproach, when to speak is a duty. No one has raised a voice in behalf of the orphan child, while several have spoken against her claim. I rise, sirs, in behalf of no common cause; liberty was its foundation, heroism and martyrdom consecrated it. I speak of **'The Orphan Child**

of the Alamo.' None, save her, can say: **'I Am the Child of the Alamo.'**

"Well do I remember the consternation that propagated throughout the land in the wake of the sad tidings that the Alamo had fallen! It was there that a gallant few threw themselves between the settlements and the enemy, and swore never to surrender or to retreat.

"They redeemed their pledge with the forfeit of their lives. And fell the self-chosen sacrifice upon the alter of Texas freedom.

"Texas, unapprised of the advance of the invader, was sleeping and dreaming in fancied security when the alarm gun of the Alamo announced that the Attila of the West was drawing near.

"Infuriated at the resistance of Travis and his noble band, Santa Anna marshaled his hosts beneath the walls and rolled wave after wave of his charging legions against the battlements.

"After days of repeated assaults and distressful bombardments, Santa Anna took a blackened and ruined mass, the bloodstained walls of the Alamo. The noble spirits of the heroic defenders had plumed their fight to another fortress, not made with hands.

"But for the stand made at the Alamo, Texas would have been desolated to the Sabine.

"Sirs, I ask this pittance, and for whom? For the only living witness — save for her mother — of this awful tragedy, this bloodiest picture in the book of time, the bravest deed that ever glowed on the annuls of any land.

"Grant this boon! She claims it as a Christian child of the

Alamo, baptized in the blood of Davy Crockett, Jim Bowie, a Bonham, a Travis!

"To turn away would be a shame. Grant her what she asks, that she may be educated and become a worthy child of the state. That she may take the position in society to which she is entitled by the illustrious services of her father."

Bryan, wiping his dank brow with a decorative handkerchief, lowered to his seat.

Susanna, sitting sanguinely in the gallery, smiled her appreciation.

Nevertheless, though aided in his contention by the eloquent oratory of future senator, James Charles Wilson, the stoic body shook its collective head:

" Due to Susanna Bellis' unsavory reputation, it would not be morally correct to allow her daughter, Angelina Elizabeth Dickinson-Bellis, privileges reserved for our stalwart members of this society. Therefore, her request for a grant of public land and assistance is hereby denied."

An interesting note might be appropriate here: Several House Representatives sitting in judgment of the two women had been frequent visitors to the Mansion House.

Angelina would marry, have children, leave them, and eventually drift to New Orleans, where she would vigorously ply the trade of prostitution.

Here is where historical records conflict. Dates pertaining to Angelina's death have been transcribed as 1869, 1870 and 1871. This author's research has found her alive and well on those dates. Moreover, further investigation has brought to light enough evidence for considering the following account correct:

In 1876, she returned to Texas, at her mother's request, to join in festivities commemorating the state's forty years of independence.

In 1878, she was in Texas to stay.

Susanna bubbled with excitement. Her gadabout daughter was just in time to accompany her to a play.

Frank Murdock's ***Davy Crockett; Or, Be Sure You're Right, Then Go Ahead***, starring the popular character actor Frank Mayo as Davy, was in Austin for a one-night performance.

"I'm the guest of honor," her arms encircled Angelina. "Joseph doesn't want to go," she tittered, smiling fondly at her husband. "He says I'm a silly old woman."

Together, the two women — the now obese Susanna and the hardened Angelina — entered a special box in the theater. The audience rose to applaud. Susanna was thrilled by the attention. Angelina gave a slight nod.

Frank Mayo bolted onto the stage, bowed sweepingly, then waved his imitation coonskin cap with gusto at a banner painted: **SPECIAL GUEST. SUSANNA DICKINSON-HANNIG — HEROINE OF THE ALAMO**.

Susanna stood and waved back.

"How did you like the play?" asked a disheveled reporter, pushing through a surrounding swarm following the performance. The crowd, many of whom were not yet born in 1836, jostled just to get a glimpse of the woman who had known Davy Crockett.

Susanna stopped for a moment, a dream-like gaze in her eyes.

"Colonel Crockett was much taller, you know," she said finally. "Mr. Mayo must be only five feet seven or eight. But I don't understand why I was invited. The story wasn't about the Alamo..."

The two women ascended their carriage with disappointment. Susanna most of all.

Within two weeks of Susanna's death Angelina moved to Galveston, where she resumed her old profession.

She never awoke from an overdose of laudanum taken to allay the irritation induced by abnormal vaginal bleeding in 1894.

She was buried in an unmarked plot at Old City Cemetery, Galveston, Texas. An unfitting monument to "The Babe of the Alamo." [3]

Travis' slave Joe, our third survivor, fled the Mexicans while they watched their triumphant bonfires.

Wary of Santa Anna's promise of liberty, he escaped on foot toward Gonzales.

Dashing from bush to bush — in fear the Mexicans were chasing him — he was well-east of San Antonio de Béxar when he met up with Susanna, Angelina, and Ben.

Traveling wearily along, the extended little group was about 20 miles out of Gonzales on March 13th, when the distant rumblings of hooves were heard. Joe, still on foot, dove into the underbrush.

"Comanche!" he warned. "You and Ben best get to hiding."

Susanna shook her head. She was much too worn-out, too heartbroken to care.

"I would rather die one way or another," she murmured, shrugging her slight shoulders.

Ben, holding tighter to her horse's reins, started slowly toward the approaching hoof beats. His job was to escort Mrs. Dickinson to Gonzales. If he died, he would have died doing his duty.

But as the horsemen drew closer, Joe jumped from the brush.

"Texians!" he yelped.

Erastus "Deaf" Smith [4], with Henry Wax Karnes, had been sent by General Houston to check on the Alamo.

On March 11th, two Mexican ranchers living near Béxar, Andrés Barcena and Anselmo Borgara, had raced into Gonzales with a paralyzing account of the fall. Everyone was dead, they said. Santa Anna was in full force.

To quell the rising panic, Houston arrested the ranchers as spies, yet would order "Deaf" Smith to verify what he felt must be true. Travis' signal gun had been silent for five days.

Smith left for Béxar on the morning of the 13th. By evening, he was back.

Gonzales prepared for the worst. Karnes had returned earlier that afternoon with Santa Anna's frightening message. "Deaf" Smith, he said, would bring in the only survivors.

Joe, like Susanna, was catered, lavished, and questioned. And, like Susanna, this copious reception ended with his depleted store of useful knowledge.

Within months, he was back planting corn on Travis' San Felipe estate. Its executor, doubling his work to clear up Travis' numerous debts, hired him out for a dollar a day.

On April 21, 1837, he escaped the enslavement of former Texas Republic Postmaster General, John Rice Jones, Jr., who had recently acquired his ownership; riding out with a Mexican friend and two stolen horses.

Here, again, historical information differs. Some records express he was soon collared and brought back to resume his servitude. Others contend he vanished into the night, reappearing in 1875 "to live out his life quietly in Austin, Texas."

This author prefers the latter assertion; that Joe, having tolerated several vexations, had ultimately succeeded in his break for freedom.

Appendix C

Did David Crockett Surrender?

Although the events surrounding David Crockett's death are not provable either way, there are a number of problems to revisionists' contention that he meekly laid down his arms as the Alamo was overrun.

Despite several detrimental accounts marking David as among five or seven defenders who surrendered and asked clemency before execution, this author has found no conclusive evidence to substantiate the following unqualified tales of a cowardly end.

These narratives are traceable to a number of Mexican army personnel attempting to ingratiate themselves in the eyes of their government, while tainting Santa Anna's rule and disgracing the most illustrious of rebels.

General Cos, as an example, claimed to have found David hiding"in one of the rooms of the barracks after the siege, spotless and well-dressed. He identified himself [as Crockett] and told as how, while on a visit, he had accidentally got caught in the Alamo after it was too late to escape. "I brought him before my brother-in-law [Santa Anna], who immediately ordered his execution with five others."

Another version has it that General Castrillón "found six terrified rebels hiding under a mattress in a back room [of the chapel]." With a promise of protection he "gently led a venerable old man by the hand as they entered the mission courtyard. Stooped at the waist, the anciano [ancient] looked gray with shock." Castrillón had "just captured the former Congressman from the United States, David Crockett."

As the wild story continues: "Crockett lied, dodged, and denied his role in the fighting… He and the others were presented to Santa Anna, herded together like so much livestock, and shot."

According to this account, Travis' slave Joe was in attendance when Castrillón delivered the prisoners. Yet, in his many depositions, dictated to a third party, he never mentioned seeing Crockett alive after the battle.

Reporter G. Norton Galloway, tracing a story to a Mexican sergeant, provided another tale in 1886[1].

In this fanciful telling neither Crockett nor Travis were killed in the final battle, having fallen "asleep among the corpses" and gone undetected:

"… When discovered, Col. Travis gave a Mexican soldier some gold coins, and while conversing with him Cos, with whom Travis had dealt very generously when San Antonio was captured by the Americans, appeared. Cos warmly embraced Travis, and induced other Mexicans, among them General Castilion [sic] to join with him in asking Santa Anna to spare Travis' life. Then David Crockett also wearily arose to his feet among the corpses. The brutal Santa Anna was terribly enraged at the disobedience of his orders, saying 'I want no prisoners.' Col. Travis was first shot in the back. He folded his arms stiffly across his breast until a bullet pierced his neck, when he fell headlong among the dead. David Crockett fell at the first fire, his body being completely riddled with bullets."

Of all the fabrications quoted to this point, this is by far the more absurd. Anyone even remotely familiar with his life would realize David Crockett's portrayal here is utterly out of character. For him to fall asleep during a battle is in itself Ridiculous. But eyewitness reports directly following the battle discern David's body as mutilated by bayonets.

William Barret Travis is also shown entirely out of character in this bit of farce. For him to bribe a Mexican soldier in an attempt to save his own life is incredible enough. However, for Cos to embrace him goes beyond any scope of the imagination. Travis and Cos were personal enemies, stemming from past humiliating conflicts with the Mexican general.

To further dispute this yarn, reliable evidence affirms, "Travis died from a single bullet in the forehead." No additional wounds were found when his body was stripped for burning.

In 1955, Mexican antiquarian Jesús Sánchez Garza was

to publish the purported diary of Lt Colonel José Enrique de la Peña. Twenty years later, archivist Carmen Perry would translate Garza's self-published book into English as ***With Santa Anna in Texas: A Personal Narrative of the Revolution***, commencing a controversy still broiling today.

Peña, one of Santa Anna's officers during the Texas Campaign, would write on David Crockett's death:

"Some seven men had survived the general carnage and were brought before Santa Anna [by General Castrillón]. Among them was the naturalist David Crockett… Santa Anna ordered his execution… Though tortured before they were killed, these unfortunates died without complaining and without humiliating themselves before their torturers."

Immediately, history revisionists picked up this allegory and carried it along for rewriting the battle's outcome. They would hail Peña's account as the "most reliable" ever discovered.

Still, even if we were to accept Peña's writings as genuine, his observations are highly suspect.

On Travis' death, his diary reported:

"They had bolted and reinforced the doors [of the Long Barrack], but in order to form trenches they had excavated some places that were now a hindrance to them. Not all of them took refuge, for some remained in the open, looking at us before firing, as if dumbfounded at our daring. Travis was seen to hesitate, but not about the death he would choose. He would take a few steps and stop, turning his proud face toward us to discharge his shots, he fought like a true soldier. Finally, he died, but he died after having traded his life very dearly. None of his men died with greater heroism, and they all died. Travis behaved as a hero, one must do him justice, for with a handful of men without discipline, he resolved to face men used to war and much superior in numbers, without supplies, with scarce munitions, and against the will of his subordinates. He was a handsome blond, with a physique as robust as his spirit was strong."

Peña, of course, mistakenly defined Travis in this piece, which brings up a troubling concern. If Peña were unable to identify Travis, wouldn't he have had difficulty singling out Crockett, since he knew none of the defenders on sight?

Travis manservant Joe stated he saw his master "fire his shotgun only once, then [he] was killed by a single shot to the forehead and died where he fell on the north wall." This was the vicinity in which his body was found.

Joe further stipulated the "venerable old man" captured by General Castrillón was a defender named "Warner [2]."

There is a possibility this Warner, whom Joe described as "a weak old man," desperately identified himself as Crockett, reasoning that posing as a United States Congressman would shield him from certain death.

So here is this author's belief: Other than Peña's questionable words for Crockett's surrender and subsequent execution, there is no credible evidence to make it so. Discerning research points to Crockett possibly dying as described in this work. The area depicted, too, is conceivably correct. This was near the section originally assigned to Crockett and his "Tennessee boys," making it improbable for them to have withdrawn inside the Long Barrack. Such a move would have exposed them to a three-way fire from the Mexicans coming in from the north wall,the southwest corner of the west wall, and from those coming over the southeast palisade. To retreat to the chapel would have been equally impractical. The Tennesseans would have had to turn their backs on the encroaching enemy to enter the church. Even if they were to attempt a dash for it, the heavy oak doors, by this time in the fighting, were barred from the inside. This, in itself, would dispute any claim of David Crockett "hiding in a back room of the chapel."

At this writing forensic study has revealed Peña's diary not a 20th century forgery, as was once thought. However, there is still no evidence against a 19th century sham. Peña dictated his recollections of the Alamo siege to a cellmate while a political prisoner in 1839, in which he never mentioned David Crockett as one of those executed by order of Santa Anna. These recountings could have been expanded and enlivened over the years, then presented as the words of Lt. Colonel José Enrique de la Peña.

There were also claims David Crockett, having begged for his life, survived the Alamo altogether and dispatched to work in the mines of Mexico.

In 1840, John Wesley Crockett, then a Congressman for Tennessee's 12th district, would investigate a report that his father was held prisoner in the Salina salt mines near Guadalajara.

It was a hoax. The man claiming he was the famous David Crockett from the Alamo admitted lying to draw attention to prisoner plights in Mexico.

Still, given the public's general sympathy on reading of David "Davy" Crockett's survival, the ruse might possibly have succeeded had the impostor been an American.

Even Jim Bowie's spirit could not escape disparaging inventions.

One story has him "cowering under the bedcovers like a woman when our brave soldiers came into the room."

In another spectacular tale Andrea Castañón Villanueva (Madame Candelaria), who claimed to have attended Bowie in his last illness, said she received "two wounds while shielding Señor Bowie from the Mexican soldiers with my body."

On a later occasion Madame Candelaria, apparently never relating the same story twice, said Bowie "died of pneumonia the day before the [final] battle of the Alamo."

But one of the most gruesome pieces of fancy pertaining to Bowie's termination comes from a newspaper article, in which its writer places credit to an eyewitness report by an unidentified Mexican soldier:

"When the pile of Texian bodies were about to be ignited, soldados brought out a cot upon which lay a sick man whom our captain identified as 'no other than the infamous Bowie.' This invalid rebel then insulted us in excellent Castillion which drove us to spread-eagle him, split open his mouth, cut out his tongue, and throw him alive into the flaming funeral pyre."

Such ghastly creativity should be left to authors of gothic horror.

Less imaginative witnesses testified Bowie's mutilated body was "found on a cot in the Low Barracks, just east of the main [south] gate. Three Mexican soldiers lay on the floor." No mention of Madame Candelaria having been near the cot, or even in the room, has ever been documented [3].

Decisively, notwithstanding the numerous volumes of tales and myths generated over one hundred and seventy years and counting, the strongest evidence that David Crockett did not surrender, or that Jim Bowie lived up to his legend and William Barret Travis his own expectations, emanates from Santa Anna himself; by his silence.

In his triumphant report after the battle, he simply said:

"… Among the corpses are those of Bowie and Travis… and also that of Crockett…"

Had any of these celebrated defenders turned craven he would have, in his self-assertive manner, been the first to give it wide publicity.

Appendix D

Was The Battle of the Alamo Really Necessary?

To military "experts" and critics, defending the Alamo at all costs was a ludicrous decision. Yet, the symbolism it manifested far transcended a strategic standpoint.

As "Remember the Alamo!" reverberated throughout the world, an echo against oppression arose in the knowledge that mankind could face subversion and accept it as the value of freedom.

What really motivated the remaining defenders to give up their lives, we may never know. That they did, though it may forever find room for debate by the experts, we should all be grateful.

Had they not taken their imperishable stand in the early days of 1836, Texas' struggle for independence would never have culminated in victory. Santa Anna would have swept to the core of her existence, laying waste to everything within his path. And General Houston would not have been able to assemble his forces, even months later, to halt the incursion.

Autonomy as a quest of mankind would also have been heavily afflicted; for Antonio López de Santa Anna intended not only to overthrow Texas, but the entire western hemisphere…

… And beyond.

That freedom owes life to the Alamo, we may be certain.

That the spirit of man owes life to her defenders, there shall never be a doubt.

Earliest known photograph (daguerreotype) taken of the Alamo shortly after the battle. The southeast palisade (David Crockett and his "Tennessee boys' " position) is to the right in the photo. (Photo courtesy: Center for American History, University of Texas at Austin.)

Enrique Esparza, age 74
(1828–1917)

As an 8-year-old boy during the siege, he was the only Alamo survivor to recount his experience in detail as the years passed. (Photo courtesy: Texas State Library and Archives Commission.)

Susanna Dickinson-Hannig
(1814–1883)

After decades of a bittersweet existence following the Alamo siege, she found certain serenity during her closing years. (Photo courtesy: Texas State Library and Archives Commission.)

Angelina Elizabeth Dickinson
(1834–1894)

Affectionately called "The Babe of the Alamo," Angelina ended her days as a prostitute. (Photo courtesy: Texas State Library and Archives Commission.)

Erastus "Deaf" Smith
(1787–1837)

Though hearing impaired, "Deaf" Smith was General Sam Houston's ablest scout during the Texas Revolution.

On March 13, 1836, he met and returned Susanna Dickinson and her little party to Gonzales. (Image courtesy: Texas State Library and Archives Commission.)

The ruined Alamo chapel as it appeared in 1846.

Three years later, the U.S. Army reclaimed the chapel, cleaned out the debris left by Santa Anna's ineffectual orders for his troops to destroy the entire complex before departing San Antonio, added the famous hump to its façade, and began using it as a warehouse. The Long Barrack, too, was put into service for storage and the sheltering of horses. (Sketch prior to his watercolor in 1847 by: Edward Everett (1818–1903). Courtesy: Amon Carter Museum, Ft. Worth, Texas.)

Dr. Rufus C. Burleson
Leading Pastor and Educator
(1823–1901)

Through his pastoral work, Dr. Burleson was instrumental in saving a wayward Susanna Dickinson (Bellis) further heartbreak and humiliation. (Image courtesy: Texas State Library and Archives Commission.)

With the fall of the Alamo the ruined chapel building and walls were deserted and left to crumble. The Roman Catholic, in 1842, resumed control and attempted to restore it as a place of worship, but could not raise the needed funds. In 1849, the U.S. Army rented the property and restored the chapel, constructing the rounded top to its façade familiar to us today. The above photograph was taken between 1850 and 1860, when the U.S. Army used the Alamo as a warehouse before the Civil War. Following the Civil War, her grounds reverted to the Catholic Church through the United States Government and the U.S. Army continued to lease the property as a depot until 1876. (Photo courtesy: Daughters of the Republic of Texas, Alamo Library, San Antonio, Texas.)

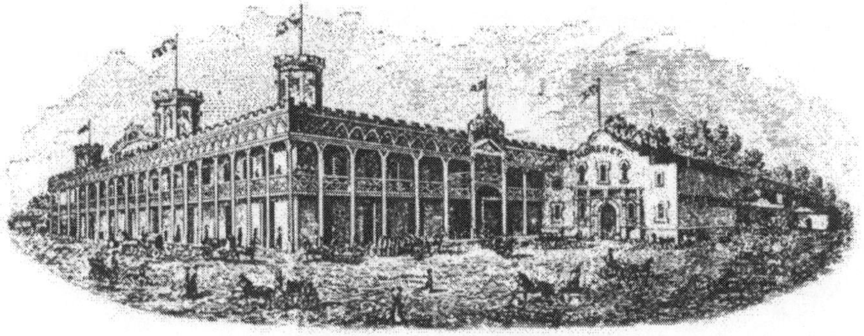

THE ALAMO AS REPAIRED BY GRENET.

In 1876, the U.S. Army decamped the Alamo for Fort Sam Houston and the Catholic Church sold the mission [Long Barrack] to Honore Grenet for $20,000. Grenet, a French-born San Antonio merchant, constructed a two-story wooden building atop the Long Barrack and operated a general store, called the "Palace," until his death in 1882. Grenet's estate sold it to the mercantile firm of Hugo & Schmeltzer at auction for $28,000 in 1886. The Catholic Church, which retained ownership of the Alamo chapel throughout the years, had sold the famous building three years earlier to the state of Texas for $20,000.

Both the Long Barrack and chapel were in danger of destruction and ruin until Adina de Zavala and Clara Driscoll set to work as saviors of the structures in 1893. (Artwork: Adina de Zavala, ***History and Legends of the Alamo***, 1917. Courtesy: Daughters of the Republic of Texas.)

Adina de Zavala
(1861–1955)

In 1893, a San Antonio group of preservationist woman headed by Adina de Zavala, granddaughter of the Mexican-born vice-president of the Republic of Texas, Lorenzo de Zavala, Jr., affiliated with the Daughters of the Republic of Texas, making the conservation of the Alamo one of its goals.

The "Daughters", led by Clara Driscoll, supported de Zavala's plan to emphasize the Texas Revolution period, with the Alamo chapel as the principal structure. Although they would later have their differences, both ladies worked things out to everyone's satisfaction. (Photo courtesy: Texas State Library and Archives Commission.)

Juan Nepomuceno Seguín Home

Photograph of famous Alamo courier (Captain) Juan Seguín and his parent's home, Casa Blanca, near Floresville, Texas, before its demolishment in the 1930s. (Photo courtesy: Library of Congress.)

Rear view of the Alamo grounds during demolition of neighboring buildings in preparation for reconstruction in 1937, as seen from the Historic Crockett Hotel. (Photo courtesy: San Antonio Light Collection, University Institute of Texas Cultures of San Antonio, 801 S. Bowie St., San Antonio, Texas.)

Excavations of the Alamo's west wall in 1979-80 revealed the two-room family residence of defender José Toribio Losoya. (Photo courtesy: Center for Archaeological Research, The University of Texas at San Antonio, One UTSA Circle, San Antonio, Texas.)

The Alamo chapel before renovations to stabilize and preserve her had been initiated in 1995, which effectively addressed the influences of time and climactic conditions on the 250-year-old edifice. (Photo courtesy: Texas State Library and Archives Commission.)

Miscellaneous

Freedom

Chapter Notes

Part One

Ancestral Past, Birth...and Adventures

Chapter 1:

1. Overflowing of a river or stream by melting snow or heavy rain.

Chapter 2:

1. The hostile Creek Indians. So-called because they painted their war clubs scarlet.
2. Davy Crockett shared whatever provisions he could with the other volunteers.
3. Andrew Jackson's letter to Rachel Jackson.
4. From General Jackson's official report after the battle.
5. So-called because it represented a sacred meeting lo-

cale for the Indians. According to an ancient legend, no white man could violate it and live.

Part Two
Sadness, Politics...and Congress

Chapter 5:

1. James Knox Polk, 11th President of the United States.
2. Crockett purposely demoted Arnold from Major General to the generic rank bestowed on elderly southern gentlemen. This in itself was comical, since Arnold (1795–1833) was younger than his opponent.

Chapter 6:

1. President Jackson was considered "the government" during his terms in office.
2. Here, we notice a refined swing in David Crockett's congressional speeches, since he read them exactly as written by Thomas Chilton.
3. When Martin Van Buren, nicknamed "Old Kinderhook (or "OK") for his birthplace, Kinderhook, New York, was president (1837–1841). He was the first president born an American citizen (1782–1862).
4. Actually written by Mathew St. Clair Clark, a disgruntled clerk in the Whig Party.
5. Contrary to some erroneous reports, this was not the "Betsy" brought to Texas by David Crockett.

Part Three

The Alamo, Death…and Victory

Chapter 7:

1. John Wesley Crockett (1807–1852) would follow his father into the political arena. In 1841, as a Congressman from Tennessee, he pushed through the land bill straddled by Adams' administration and discarded by Jackson's.
2. The Washington press, to deride Crockett for his treatment of President Jackson, invented this story. At first David denied it, but the public loved him for it. Other sources place its conception with Thomas Chilton. In either case, David milked it for all it was worth.
3. It is not entirely clear as to the "Son & Daughter" written to. However, what remains a mystery is why David did not address this letter to his wife.
4. She was then Mrs. Isabelle Clark, wife of the founder of Clarksville (Jim Clark).
5. Actually, David wore a new fox skin cap, with the tail hanging to his shoulders, for the trip.
6. Some say the Alamo was named for the cottonwood trees, known as Los Alamos, which lined the water ditches flowing on her east and west sides, and under the walls. For the sake of accordance, both contentions may prove correct.
7. This was before Rezin, Jr. fashioned the knife that made his brother famous. England manufactured the

Bowie knife soon after for sale to the American frontier.

8. Knives were the foremost fighting weapons used in the early 1800s.
9. As a Mexican citizen Bowie was entitled to eleven leagues of land. However, optioned by his father-in-law's influence, he was allowed up to a million acres.
10. David Crockett could change his vernacular from simple backwoodsman to sophisticated speaker as the mood struck him, often baffling his listeners.
11. Gun position.
12. The only "original" part of the Alamo standing today. The Long Barrack remains as a museum, but not as it stood in 1836.
13. Dr. Amos Pollard, one of six garrison physicians.
14. Actually, the bombardment lasted no more than six hours. Travis, with his flair for dramatics, quadrupled its time for effect.
15. Although David Crockett was found not to have kept a written recounting of the siege, William Barret Travis and several others, both on the Texian and Mexican side, did. Many conversations and activities enveloped within this work were derived from these diaries.
16. Johanna Troutman fashioned a flag of silk — blue on white — with a single five-point star, subscribed "Liberty or Death." Having been first raised on January 8, 1836 in Velasco, Texas, it is believed by numerous Texans the primary flag flown.
17. The day General Gaona's troops arrived, Santa Anna

ordered another scarlet flag placed on Powder House Hill in full view of the "hated Texians."

18. No word that Texas had declared independence on March 2, 1836, ever reached the Alamo.
19. Travis had persuaded Rosanna to leave the boy with him when she visited Texas in 1835, to discuss reconciliation or divorce.
20. For decades since, historians have wrangled validity to this particular Alamo account. It is, however, this author's contention that is did occur. Perhaps not in such a dramatic manner, yet Travis did address his men (On March 5th, not on the March 3rd of earlier writings.), and all but one (Louis Moses Rose) chose to remain.

    At any rate, Travis's speech and his drawing the line is part of the Alamo legend. And, as one famous publisher once noted: "When fact disputes legend, print the legend."
21. Some chroniclers accord Jim Bowie a Negro slave named Sam (or sometimes Ham). However, historical records fail to produce any evidence that Bowie owned such a slave before entering the Alamo.

    There is also no record of a Negro dying by Bowie's cot (as depicted in certain books and movies), or that a Sam (Ham) ever spoke of surviving the Alamo. He simply vanished from nonfiction history.

    "Sam" or "Ham" was actually Colonel Almonte's American Negro orderly, Ben, who accompanied Susanna Dickinson to Sam Houston after the Alamo's fall.

22. Despite traditional portraits of William Barret Travis wearing a uniform at the Alamo siege, he actually wore homespun trousers and a Texas jersey jacket.
    Although he had ordered a uniform from tailors McKinney and Williams in December or early January of 1836, it was not ready when he left for the Alamo on January 23rd.
23. Conventional history records the siege as lasting 13 days, yet the battle itself took place for 12 days.
24. "No surrender, boys!"
25. Napoléon Bonaparte was Santa Anna's idol. He even mimicked Bonaparte's stance while pondering; his right hand pressed inside his tunic, with his left hand behind his back. (Napoléon I, 1759–1821. Emperor of France, 1804–1815.)
26. From a rollicking, if somewhat risqué, tune of the day:

    Will you come into my bow'r I have shaded for you? Our bed shall be roses all spangled with dew. There under the bow'r on roses you'll be.
    With a blush on your cheeks, but a smile in Your eye.

27. No one knows for sure which flag anchored the Alamo during the siege. It may have been the Mexican tri-color with the date "1824" set in the middle, denoting reinstatement of the Constitution of 1824. Or the tri-color flag with two stars in the middle marking ***Coahuila y Tejas***, designating the reunification of Coahuila and Texas. (Coahuila and Texas never re-

united. Texas eventually became the state of Texas, while Coahuila would form the short-lived Republic of the Rio Grande.)

Or a half dozen other flags, including the one bought by Travis for five dollars en route to the Alamo.

Then again, it may yet be the azure blue flag of the New Orleans Greys — torn from the roof of the Long Barrack — who took an independent stand from the beginning. As of this writing, that flag resides in the National Museum, Chapultepic Castle, Mexico City.

At any rate the flag, which stood in defiance at the Alamo, is an issue still unresolved.

28. This witness is believed today to have been Ramón Caro, Santa Anna's civilian secretary.
29. Gregorio Esparza was spared cremation by his brother Francisco, a soldier under Santa Anna, who begged for his body. He was laid to rest in the old Campo Santo Cemetery, San Antonio de Béxar.
30. Elizabeth Patton Crockett died at the age of 72, in Granbury, Hood County, Texas, and was interred in what is now known as Acton State Historic Site. Texas' smallest state park.

    Above her grave stands a 28-foot marble monument, erected in 1911, featuring a bonneted frontierswoman with a hand shading her eyes as she looks toward the west, forever wondering when her husband will come home.

Epilogue:

1. In 1889, shortly before his death, Juan Seguín stated

he buried the coffin near the steps of San Fernando Church, Béxar.

In 1936, a work detail repairing the cathedral's altar railing unearthed a box containing charred bones with shreds of uniforms and buttons, leading to a controversy persisting to this day.

Many historians believe the remains discovered are those of the Alamo defenders. Others do not, including this author.

Reason?

None of the defenders wore military garb, not even Colonel Travis. Furthermore, the bodies were stripped prior to burning.

2. Actually by Cos' cannon when he occupied the fort in December of 1835.

Appendix A:

1. Outside research may add to the roster in the future. Some historians believe the count nearer to 250.
2. James M. Rose was a nephew of James Madison, 4th President of the United States.
3. Believed to have been a former slave of Francis L. Desauque, who entered the Alamo when his master was dispatched from Béxar for supplies on or about February 22nd.

   John and several unknown blacks banded together to bare arms and die in the final battle.

   Francis Desauque, unable to make it back before the Alamo fell, would die in the Goliard massacre of March 27, 1836.

Appendix B:

1. Pamelia Mann owned the Mansion House from 1837 until her death from yellow fever in 1840.
2. At the age of 15, Guy Bryon was one of the couriers who helped spread Travis' "Victory or Death" message.

   On March 4, 1836, he delivered his copy to Velasco, Texas.
3. Although the date, place and circumstance of Angelina's death have been uncertain for years, careful research has discarded the 1870 date recorded by her "family historians."

   Too, the obituary in Galveston's ***Flake's Daily Bulletin*** of July 1869, which refers to her as "Em Britton, daughter of Mrs. Robertson, who were saved at the Alamo," is subject to question.

   There was no Mrs. Robertson at the Alamo, nor has deep probing placed an "Em" or "Emma" as the child of a Mrs. Robertson. There was a defender named James Waters Robertson, who was married to a Sarah Carson. Sarah did not accompany her husband to Texas, but remained in her home state of Louisiana throughout the revolution. They had no children.

   Old City Cemetery, Galveston, Galveston County, Texas records an "Angelina Elizabeth Dickinson buried in an unmarked plot. Date of death unknown." This author, for lack of further information, has computed her year of death as 1894. No records show an "Em Britton" interred in any of Galveston County's ten cemeteries examined.

Therefore, we must reach the conclusion that Angelina Dickinson and Em Britton were different individuals. They may have known each other in life; yet, in death, they were separate.

4. Erastus "Deaf" Smith, if somewhat hard of hearing, was Sam Houston's ablest scout in Texas' fight for independence.

Appendix C:

1. "Sketch of San Antonio," G. Norton Galloway. ***Magazine of American History***, vol. 25, no. 6, June 1886.
2. Historical registers list a Thomas S. Warner as a possible Alamo victim. However, we only have Joe's word he was the "weak old man" described. To date, Warner has not been officially credited as an Alamo defender.
3. When Madame Candelaria made her claim to have been in the Alamo during the siege, Susanna Dickinson testified she was not. Whereupon, Madame Candelaria angrily countered: "Mrs. Dickinson is a racist and hates Mexicans."

   If this were true, why would Susanna vouch for Gregorio Esparza's wife and family, and other Mexican survivors, when their claims were made.

   Juana Alsbury attended Bowie's illness during the siege.

   On February 12, 1891, eight years prior to her death at the age of 113, the Texas State Legislature would award Madame Candelaria a pension of twelve dollars a month to relieve itself of her claims.

Miscellaneous Notes:

On David Crockett's Death

(a) Sergeant Felix Nunez of the Mexican army would describe the actions of a man identified only as a member of the force defending the southwest palisade:

"He was a **tall** American of rather dark complexion and had on a long buckskin coat and a round cap without any bill, with a long tail hanging down his back. This man apparently had a charmed life. Of the soldados who took deliberate aim at him and fired, not one ever hit him. On the contrary, he never missed his mark. He killed at least eight of our men, besides wounding several others.

"This being observed by a lieutenant, who had come over the wall, he sprang at him and dealt him a deadly blow with his sword, just above the right eye, which felled him to the ground. In an instant, he was pierced by not less than 20 bayonets."

Detractors would discount Nunez's depiction, which sounded suspiciously like David Crockett, on the argument that the frontiersman was "no more than five feet eight and of stocky build."

This author, however, has placed Crockett at 6′ 3″ and proportionally built for his height. This determination results from the study of portraits of him throughout his life, including a full-size painting observed in the lobby of the Historic Crockett Hotel adjacent to the Alamo in 2001.

None show him as stocky.

It has also been seen, in full-length representations positioned next to a "long rifle," that he stood at least nine inches above the weapon's barrel-end, while the butt rested on the ground. The Kentucky Long Rifle, David Crockett's preferred firearm, averaged five feet-five inches from butt to barrel-end.

(b) Colonel Almonte's orderly, Ben, having seen Congressman Crockett while employed by a hotel in Washington City, was called into the fort to identify his body.

Ben reported seeing "…it surrounded by about sixteen Mexicans, a knife stuck in one."

On Jim Bowie's Death

When Bowie's mother was informed of her son's death, she simply commented: "I'll wager they found no wounds in his back."

On Susanna Dickinson

Susanna Dickinson always believed her friend, Mrs. Ramón Musquíz, intervened with Santa Anna to save the lives of the Alamo women and children.

When Mrs. Musquíz, wife of Béxar Mexican official Ramón Musquíz who was friendly to the Texian position, heard of Santa Anna's desire to annihilate the entire fort, she went to the general with a plea to "spare Mrs. Dickinson and her child."

In weighing the pros and cons to this entreaty, he hesitently promised no women and children in the fort would be harmed intentionally.

"If we could read the secret history of our enemies, we should find in each person's life sorrow and suffering to disarm all hostility."

Henry Wadsworth Longfellow
(1807–1882)

David Crockett and Texas Facts

Did You Know:

Rebecca Hawkins (1756–1834), mother of David Crockett, was descended from St. Francis Xavier (1506–1556) through the marriage of her sister Sarah (? –1780) to John Sevier (1745–1815), 1st governor of Tennessee.

In 1816, while exploring Alabama land, Davy Crockett contracted malaria and lay along a road near death. Surprisingly, he recovered and returned to Tennessee and family. When his wife remarked of his reported death, he grinningly replied, "Betsy, I know'd that wuz a whopper of a lie, as soon as I heard it."

Named by Andrew Edwards Gossett (1812–1890) for his father's friend and former Tennessee neighbor, Crockett, Texas is the county seat for Houston County, the first county established by the republic.

Although Texian hero James "Jim" Bowie's name was well-known during his lifetime, his legend did not begin until 1852, when a widely circulated 19th century magazine on the American south called ***DeBow's Review*** published a fabricated article written by his brother, John Jones Bowie.

Western humorist Will Rogers' (1879–1935) grandfather and great uncle were youthful friends of Sam Houston. Their half-sister, Rogers' great aunt Diana (Indian name: Tiana, ca 1796–1838), was Sam Houston's Cherokee wife.

The first Indians, called Paleo-Indians, entered (Texas') territorial land around 10,000 B.C.E.

The word Texas (or Tejas) stems from the Spanish pronunciation of a Caddo Indian word for "friends" or "allies.

Lubbock, located in the northeastern section of Lubbock County, Texas is the site of one of the oldest areas of human inhabitants in North America, dating back some 12,000 years to the Clovis period.

General Sam Houston carried only two books with him throughout the Texas Revolution, ***Caesar's War Commentaries*** and ***Gulliver's Travels***.

Five sites served as temporary Texas capitals in 1836: Washington-on-the-Brazos (now a ghost town), Harrisburgh (now Harrisburg), Galveston, Velasco, Columbia (presently West Columbia). In 1837, the capital was moved to Houston by order of Sam Houston, then to its permanent residence in the new town of Austin in 1839.

When Texas was annexed in 1845, she retained the right to fly her Lone Star flag at the same height as the national flag; due to the fact she officially entered the United States by treaty and not territorial annexation.

Texas is the only state to have had flags of six different nations hoisted above her: Spain, 1519–1685, 1690–1821;

France, 1685–1690; Mexico, 1821–1836; Republic of Texas, 1836–1845; United States, 1845–1861; Confederate States, 1861–1865; United States, 1865–present.

On May 14, 1854, German delegates living in western Texas met in San Antonio to declare slavery an evil entity, which led many Anglo-Texans to mistrust their Germanic neighbors when Texas joined the Confederacy in 1861.

Milton Murray Holland (1844–1910), a freed slave, was the first Texan Medal of Honor recipient (issued April 6, 1865) for his courage as a sergeant major in the 5th United States Colored Troops during the Civil War.

Milton M. Holland
(1844–1910)
Medal of Honor Citation:
"Took command of Company C,
after all the officers had been killed or wounded,
and gallantly led it."
Photo courtesy: Library of Congress.

The last battle of the Civil War was fought on May 12–13, 1865 at Palmito Ranch, near Brownsville, Texas, more than a month after the surrender of General Robert E. Lee at Appomattox Court House, Virginia, culminating in a Confederate victory.

The first powered flying machine was flown in Texas in 1865, nearly forty years before the Wright brothers' famous flight of 1903.

Teacher and inventor Jacob Friedrich Brodbeck (1821–1910) powered the plane with coil springs, reaching treetop heights before crashing into a henhouse.

Though several lay claim, the first hamburger was created in Athens, Texas in the late 1880s by Fletcher "Old Dave" Davis (1864–1941), operator of a café at 115 Tyler Street, Henderson County, on the north side of the courthouse square.

Later, Davis would vend his innovation at the St. Louis World's Fair of 1904. He and his wife set up on the fair's midway as "Old Dave's Hamburger Stand."

Today, residents of Texas usually refer to themselves as Texans. However, the handle Texian had been sporadically used as late as 1880 — thirty-five years after originally entering the Union.

Austin's historic Driskill Hotel is well known as one of the most haunted lodges in the United States. It is said that a celebrated resident spirit roams the 5th floor hall, nodding politely to guests before vanishing.

"Texas, Our Texas," written and composed by William J Marsh and Gladys Yoakum Wright, was adopted as Texas' official state song by winning a contest in 1929.

Houston is the largest Texas city by population. (2,229, 199, as of this writing)

Fort Hood, located in Killeen, central Texas, is the largest military base in the world. (349 square miles, as of this writing)

Howard Hughes (1905–1976), once the world's most eccentric billionaire, was born in Humble, Texas.

Abilene, Texas' surrounding area is so oil-rich, when the

city erected a rig in 1981 at its county fairgrounds to demonstrate use of the oil drilling equipment it struck oil!

"Texas is neither southern nor western. Texas is Texas!"
Senator William Arvis "Dollar Bill" Blakely
(1898–1976)

Bibliography

No historical effort can ever begin without extensive research of its subject. Whether we agree with past renderings is irrelevant, since it is left to the present author to garner whatever material found available and return a final determination as to its reliability.

The following represents but a small portion of the numerous books, articles and papers examined during preparation of this work. Though some are a matter for dispute, all have been explored in an attempt for an accurate analysis.

And, this author feels sure, any shortcomings on his part will find themselves redressed in future portrayals.

Allen, Charles Fletcher. ***David Crockett, Scout: Small Boy, Pilgrim, Soldier, Bear-Hunter, and Congressman Defender of the Alamo***. National Book Network, 2001.

Alsbury, Juana. "Mrs. Alsbury's Recollections of the Alamo." John Ford Papers, Texas University Press Archives.

Baugh, Virgil E. ***Rendezvous at the Alamo: Highlights in the Lives of Bowie, Crockett and Travis***. University of Nebraska Press, 2003.

Burke, James Wakefield. ***David Crockett: The Man Behind the Myth***. Eakin Press, 1984.

Clariton, Wallace O. ***Exploring the Alamo Legends***. Rowman & Littlefield Publications, Inc., 1998.

Cobia, Manley F. ***Journey into the Land of Trials: The Story of Davy Crockett's Expedition to the Alamo***. Providence House Publishers, 2003.

Coles, Henry L. ***The War of 1812***. University of Chicago Press, 1965.

Davis, Burke. ***Old Hickory: A Life of Andrew Jackson***. Dial Press, 1977.

Davis, William C. ***Three Roads to the Alamo: The Lives and Fortunes of David Crockett, James Bowie, and William Barret Travis***.

HarperCollins, Publishers, 1999.

Derr, Mark. ***The Frontiersman: The Real Life and Legends of Davy Crockett***. Morrow Press, 1993.

Dobie, Frank. "Jim Bowie, Big Dealer." Southwestern Historical Quarterly (hereafter cited as S.H.Q.), 60, No. 3, January 1957.

Flanagan, Sue. ***Sam Houston's Texas***. University of Texas Press, 1964.

Fradin, Dennis B. ***The Alamo***. Benchmark Publishing, 2006.

Groneman, Bill. ***Eyewitness to the Alamo***. Republic of Texas Press, 1996.

Habig, Marion A. ***The Alamo Mission: San Antonio de Velaro, 1718–1793***. Francisco Herald Press, 1968.

Hanson, Todd, Editor. ***The Alamo Reader: A Study in History***. Stackpole Books, 2003.

Hardin, Stephen L. ***Alamo 1836: Santa Anna's Texas Campaign***. Greenwood Publishing Group, Inc., 2004.

Hardin, Stephen L. "A Volley from the Darkness: Sources Regarding the Death of William Barret Travis." The Alamo Journel, December 1987.

Holland, James W. "Andrew Jackson and the Creek War: Victory at Horseshoe Bend." Alabama Review, October 1968.

Huneycutt, C.D. ***At the Alamo: Captain Navarro's Memoirs***. Gold Star Press, 1988.

James, Marquis. ***The Raven: A Biography of Sam Houston***. Bobbs-Merrill, 1929.

Johnson, James R. ***The Alamo: Heroes and Myths***. J.G. Burke, Publisher, 2005.

Kilgore, Dan. ***How Did Davy Die?*** Texas A & M University Press, 1978.

King, Richard. ***Susanna Dickinson: Messenger of the Alamo***. Shoal Creek Publications, 1976.

Kuyendall, James H. "Remembrances of Early Texans." S.H.Q., Vol. 7, No. 1, July 1903.

Leckie, Robert. ***Great Battles of American History***. Random House, 1968.

Lindley, Thomas Ricks. ***Alamo Traces: New Evidences and New Conclusions***. Taylor Trade Publishing, 2006.

McDonald, Archie P. ***Travis***. Jenkins Publishing, 1968.

Miller, Thomas Lloyd. ***Bounty and Donation Land Grants of Texas, 1835 –1888***. University of Texas Press, 1968.

Nelson, Kristen L. ***El Alamo/the Alamo***. Lerner Publishing Group, 2005.

Presley, James. "Santa Anna in Texas: A Mexican Viewpoint." S.H.Q., Vol. 62, No.4, July 1959.

Quackenbush, Robert. ***Quit Pulling My Leg: A Story of Davy Crockett***. Prentice-Hall, 1987.

Ragsdale, Crystal Sasse. ***The Women and Children of the Alamo***. Texas A & M University Press, 1994.

Rosenberg, Charles. ***The Cholera Years: The United States in 1832, 1849, and 1866***. University of Chicago Press, 1962.

Schlesinger, Arthur M., Jr. ***The Age of Jackson***. Brown, Little, 1945.

Shackford, James Atkins. ***David Crockett: The Man and the Legend***. University of North Carolina Press, 1956.

Sibley, Marilyn McAdams. "The Burial Place of the Alamo Heroes." S.H.Q., Vol. 70, No. 2, October 1966.

Smith, Richard Penn. ***On to the Alamo: Colonel Crockett's Exploits and Adventures in Texas***. Editor: John Seelye, Penguin USA, Publishing, 2003.

Tinkle, Lon. ***Thirteen Days to Glory: The Siege of the Alamo***. McGraw-Hill, 1958.

Turner, Margaret Ann. ***William Barret Travis: His Sword and his Pen***. Texas Press, 1965.

Williams, Amelia. "A Critical Study of the Siege of the Alamo and the Personnel of its Defenders." S.H.Q., Vol. 36, Nos. 3–9, April – October 1933 and Vol. 37, Nos. 1–4, January–April 1934.

Williams, Amelia. "Notes on Alamo Survivors." S.H.Q. Vol 49, No. 4, April 1946.

Index

An italicized *n* following a page number is a chapter note.

A

Index

B

Index

Index

Index

Index

Index

Index

D

Index

E

F

Index

Index

Index

Index

J

K

Index

L

Index

Index

N

O

P

Q

Index

R

S

Index

T

Index

Index

U

V

Index

W

About the Author

Dr. Bouffard holds an LL.B. from LaSalle University, a Masters and Psy.D.. from Neotarian College of Psychology. And has applied thirty years to psychological counseling.

In 1999, he earned a Ph.D. (a candidacy shelved for twenty years due to time restraints) in Theocentric Business and Ethics from American College of Metaphysical Theology, leading to ministerial credentials.

His lifelong fascination with history has led him to currently author several papers and books in this genre.

16148445R00213

Made in the USA
Middletown, DE
06 December 2014